SEP 13 1999

[FRAYSER

OUTDOOR PLAY

~~~~~~~~~~

Written by Ellen Moshein

Illustrated by Kelly McMahon

Photography by Anthony Nex

FS-32601 Outdoor Play
All rights reserved—Printed in the U.S.A.
Copyright ©1997 Frank Schaffer Publications, Inc.
23740 Hawthorne Blvd.
Torrance, CA 90505

Notice! Copies of student pages may be reproduced by the teacher for home or classroom use only, not for commercial resale. No part of this publication may be reproduced for storage in a retrieval system, or transmitted in any form or by any means—electronic, mechanical, recording, etc.—without the prior written permission of the publisher. Reproduction of these materials for an entire school system is strictly prohibited.

Table of Contents

Introduction	1–2
Classroom Management	3–8
Warmups	9–10
Stretching	11–15
Team Games	**16–34**
Kickball	17
Basketball	20
Flag Football	23
Soccer	26
Softball	29
Volleyball	32
Cooperative Games	**35–62**
Balloon Dodge Ball	36
Crazy Cones	37
Double Ball Toss	38
Dragon's Tail	39
Hop Sticks	40
Jumper Ball	41
Leapfrog	42
Man in the Middle	43
Mirrors	44
Pinball Soccer	45
Shark and Minnows	46
Steal the Bacon	47
Beach Towel Volleyball	48
Cars	49
Crab Soccer	50
Group Juggling	51
Long Jump Ropes	52
One Step	53
Pickle	54
Submarine Tag	55
Zigzag Kickball	56
Balloon Volleyball	57
Barrel Ball Basketball	58
Blanketball	59
Crows and Cranes	60
Grass Drills	61
Ultimate Handball	62
Relays	**63–80**
Animal Relays	64
Around the Bases Relay	66
Hula-Hoop Relay	67
Change Leaders	68
Continuous Passing Relay	69
Dribble Relay	70
Kangaroo Relay	71
Long-distance Relay	72
Over-Under	73
Pony Express Relay	74
Suitcase Relay	75
Ten Free Throws	76
Time Bomb	77
Total Movement Relay	78
Train Relays	79
Pass and Duck Relay	80
Individual Fitness Activities	**81–104**
Around the Block	82
Freeze Dance	83
Hula-Hoops	84
In, Out, and Around	85
Jump and Jog	86
Jump Ropes	87
Jump the River	88
Shuttle Run	89
Aerobics	90
Fitness Circuits	93
Name Game	94
Obstacle Courses	95
Track and Field	96
Sportsfest	98
Bowling	101
Racket Skills	104
Playground Games	**105–113**
Handball	106
Roly-poly	107
Tetherball	108
Four Corners	109
Foursquare	110
Hopscotch	111
Prisoner	112
Spud	113
Parachute Activities	**114–118**
Awards and Forms	**119–126**
What Are Your Physical Skills?	121
Interest Inventory	122
Team Rosters	123
Sportsmanship Award	124
Certificate of Achievement	125
Great Effort Award	126

INTRODUCTION

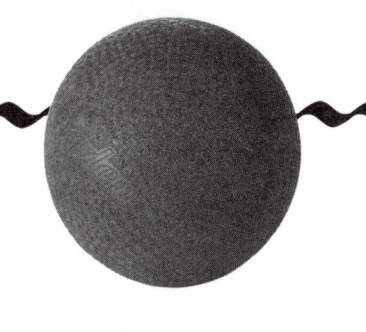

This book is intended for use as a resource for teaching physical education. The games and activities are simple to learn, simple to teach, and lots of challenging fun for the students! This book contains ideas for individual and cooperative games as well as tips on classroom management. Included in the games are several that require very little equipment but which encourage participation by every student. There is even an entire chapter devoted to activities using a classic and well-loved playground tool—the parachute. Suggestions for other noncompetitive playground activities appear throughout the book. Finally, this book provides several copies of award forms to help celebrate the students' participation and success!

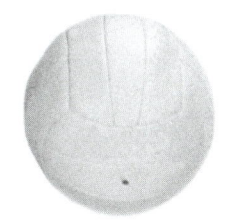

Any instructional leader can use the activities described in this book to help promote physical fitness in children. In doing so, a teacher can provide students with opportunities not only to succeed in physical education, but also to develop a lifelong commitment to the health benefits and pleasure of physical activity!

Physical education can be a useful interdisciplinary tool because it can provide an important boost to academics. Many of the skills that students learn during physical education activities directly correlate with skills they need for success in the classroom. Specifically, students learn to cooperate and communicate with each other as they participate in P.E. activities. They can develop a strong sense of camaraderie and team spirit during physical education. This, in turn, will help them rally together as a classroom. Further, these activities can help students strengthen their communications skills. As individuals working as a cooperative unit toward a common goal—as is done in a team sport—students necessarily sharpen their communication skills. Students learn how to lead, take directions, listen, and encourage one another. These are skills that transfer directly into the classroom and into the larger community.

This book is designed to assist instructors or leaders of elementary- and middle-school-aged children. Physical education at the elementary level helps students learn to work with partners and groups, share equipment, take turns, and solve problems, as they develop physical coordination. In the middle-school levels, P.E. provides students with opportunities to practice working in larger groups, to meet challenges, and to experience friendly competition.

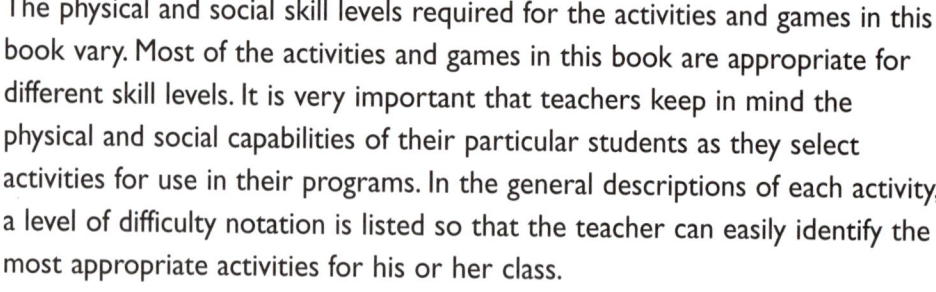

The physical and social skill levels required for the activities and games in this book vary. Most of the activities and games in this book are appropriate for different skill levels. It is very important that teachers keep in mind the physical and social capabilities of their particular students as they select activities for use in their programs. In the general descriptions of each activity, a level of difficulty notation is listed so that the teacher can easily identify the most appropriate activities for his or her class.

The lowest level of difficulty is **simple**. Activities that are labeled as simple require a minimum level of physical skills. These games also require only a minimum amount of equipment and set-up time, and have a simple set of rules. Simple activities are ideal for primary students.

The next level of difficulty is **moderate**. Activities that are labeled as moderate require an intermediate level of physical coordination and skills. These activities likewise require a moderate amount of equipment and set-up time, and have a more complicated system of rules. These games require that students are capable of understanding multiple sets of instructions and can work cooperatively in small groups.

The highest level of difficulty is **challenging**. Activities that are labeled as challenging involve high-level physical coordination, stamina, and manipulation skills. These activities often require more equipment and set-up time, and can have a complicated set of rules.

By choosing activities that are appropriate to the students' capability levels, teachers can ensure that the students will be able to achieve success during their physical education experiences. Once success on the playground is ensured, success in the classroom is not far behind!

CLASSROOM MANAGEMENT

Physical education should be a positive experience for the teacher and the students. Teaching activities outdoors should not be any more difficult than teaching in the classroom. The key to a successful lesson is establishing and maintaining control of the outdoor classroom. Making students aware of both the rules and the expectations for outdoor activities will help ensure that everyone enjoys an exciting, well-ordered outdoor learning experience.

BOUNDARIES

The first step in managing the outdoor classroom is to make sure all the students know where the boundaries of the playing area are located. Students are used to having walls around them and desks to sit in while they are inside the classroom. When the students are out on the field or playground, they must have visible boundaries. Use existing structures such as fences, tether ball poles, and backstops as boundary markers. If these are insufficient, place plastic or rubber cones around the playing area to mark the boundaries more clearly.

ESTABLISHING TEAMS

The next step in successful outdoor classroom management is to pre-establish teams for the students. The way in which this is done can vary according to class level. The teacher's leadership is essential in this process to ensure that the *playing* time is not overcome by the *planning* time.

It is important for the instructor of **primary** levels to take charge of setting up the teams in order to save valuable playing time. Having the instructor establish teams before leaving the indoor classroom will also save playing time. When the instructor establishes the teams, he or she can create a good gender balance on the teams and equally disperse the students with more athletic ability among the teams.

For the teacher of **middle** levels, it is possible to allow the students to choose their own teams as long as selections are made in a fair and equitable manner. If this is not possible, have students "count off" by number. (For example, 15 students could count off by threes to create five groups.) Then the teacher may choose or the class may vote on team captains.

Once the teams are established, give each team a number or allow the teams to give themselves team names. Keep the same team numbers or names from month to month, but shuffle students around to create new teams!

ROUTINES

To ensure that physical education classes progress efficiently, it is important to establish daily routines. At the beginning of each class, the students should go directly to the assigned playing area and line up with their teams for warmup exercises. To minimize transition time, the warmup area should be within the boundaries of the playing area to be used during the lesson. The teacher should begin the warmup by leading the students in some type of aerobic activity such as jumping jacks or jogging. Next, with the students standing an arm's-length distance apart from one another, the teacher should lead the students in stretching exercises. Older students may also lead these exercises. Appropriate warmup and stretching exercises are described on pages 9–15.

After the warmups and stretches are completed, the teacher should explain and model the skills that the students will practice for the lesson. Skill practice is an important component of the physical education program and should be completed before the students engage in playing any games. After the students have had time to practice skills, they can then participate in the planned game or activity for the day. At the conclusion of the day's lesson, have the students once again line up with their teams before being dismissed. If time permits, have the students do a few stretching exercises.

SIGNALS

It is important to implement an outdoor quiet signal. When used sparingly, a whistle can serve as an effective signal. One strong, loud whistle blow, when used at the appropriate time, should serve as an outdoor attention-getter. The students should be trained to stop, look at, and listen to the teacher as soon as the signal is given. If the students are spread out over a large playing area, they should be instructed to come in and line up in front of the teacher when they hear the whistle. Students who do not respond to signals should be disciplined according to the teacher's indoor classroom management plan.

DIRECTIONS

The instructor must give clear and explicit directions for every activity so that the students know what is expected of them. He or she should then check for understanding by asking the students to repeat the directions. While explaining directions verbally, the teacher must be sure to model expected behaviors and skills for each activity.

CREATING A LESS COMPETITIVE ATMOSPHERE

One of the most important ingredients for a successful fitness program is a noncompetitive atmosphere. Physical education class should not be about winning and losing. Nor should it be a time where some students feel intimidated, while others become overly competitive. It should be a time when all students can feel safe and secure with themselves and their own ability levels.

To achieve this atmosphere, the teacher should choose activities that are appropriate for the average skill level of the entire class. An instructor can build students' self-esteem by setting all students up for success and praising them for their efforts. One way a teacher can set the students up for success in P.E. is to avoid activities that are too difficult for the less-skilled students. If students feel confident about their abilities, they will all be more inclined to participate actively.

In order to manage competitiveness, the teacher should limit the number of games played in which teams keep score. The teacher can praise and reward individual students for such things as teamwork, positive attitudes, good sportsmanship, and effort instead of acknowledging winning teams. Giving continual positive feedback to the students during every activity and presenting awards to students for positive efforts models appropriate sportsmanship behaviors. (See pages 119–126 for achievement awards and progress forms.)

SAFETY

Another important management consideration is how to ensure the students' safety. When planning P.E. activities, consider the safety precautions that must be taken to prevent injuries and accidents. The students should be told to come to school in appropriate clothes for participating in physical education. They must wear rubber-soled shoes and loose, comfortable clothing that their parents know may get dirty. The playing area must be checked to ensure that it is free of obstacles such as holes, mud, broken glass, and other potentially dangerous objects. It is crucial for the teacher to maintain control of all activities throughout the lesson in order to ensure a safe environment. Finally, any physical problems that the students may have, such as asthma, vision and hearing problems, scoliosis, or physical injuries must be taken into account when planning and implementing a lesson.

TIME

The use of time is another important management strategy. Limit the warmup and stretching segment of the class to between 5 and 10 minutes. Transition times between activities should take less than one minute. Explaining and modeling the skills for the activity should not exceed five minutes. Allow 10 to 20 minutes for the game or activity. Finally, allow a few minutes at the end of each lesson for the students to cool down and get drinks of water. Overall, each lesson should last from 25 to 40 minutes.

Because students enjoy testing their own speed, it is also helpful to use a stopwatch to time how fast the class can respond to specific instructions, such as lining up or putting equipment away. Giving the students time frames for performing tasks is an extremely effective management tool. Have them practice these skills and challenge them to reduce the time spent on specific tasks.

AVOIDING PROBLEMS

Avoiding potential problems before they happen will lead to successful lessons. It is imperative that the teacher maintain control of the class at all times. The games should not be allowed to become overly competitive, and the students should be cautioned to follow directions at all times. Students who do not get along should be placed on different teams. A student who loses control should take a short time-out away from the class. The use of play areas and fields should be coordinated among all the teachers to avoid overcrowding and the resulting confusion. Whenever possible, the play area should be set up ahead of time with boundaries marked and equipment arranged as needed. Routines and your discipline policy must be consistent.

It is important to choose activities that involve the entire class. The teacher should plan enough variation and activity into the lesson so that students spend little—if any—time sitting and waiting for an opportunity to participate. Keep everyone involved and moving as much as possible. One way to ensure continuous student participation is to pull out small groups of students from team games to work on specific skills. For example, while one group plays a soccer game, another group works with the teacher on a drill to improve kicking skills. Music is another great way to keep students interested. There are many activities, such as jumping rope and aerobics, that can be enhanced with upbeat music to help motivate the students.

Finally, the teacher should be enthusiastic about physical fitness in general and about the activities in particular. The teacher should model skills and should participate in activities when appropriate. The teacher who gives students a love for physical activity and fitness will truly give them a gift for a lifetime.

EQUIPMENT

Having the proper equipment is another key to managing the outdoor classroom. As mentioned previously, a loud whistle and a stopwatch are important pieces of equipment for the successful physical education program. Boundary markers such as plastic or rubber cones are also a necessity. Careful planning will ensure that the necessary equipment is ready for each lesson. Try to keep the required number of balls, cones, and other equipment in a sturdy bag or small cart with a whistle, stopwatch, and paper and pencil for noting both achievement and discipline problems. Storing all P.E. materials in a separate closet or cupboard will make keeping track of the equipment easier. It is essential to keep an inventory of P.E. materials and to be sure that the balls are pumped up and clearly marked with the appropriate name or room number.

A good imagination is invaluable when it comes to acquiring equipment. It is not necessary to purchase brand new, and often expensive, equipment. If you are on a tight budget, try to solicit equipment donations.

EQUIPMENT
- stopwatch
- whistle
- plastic or rubber cones
- parachute
- tennis balls
- kickballs
- handballs
- basketballs
- soccer balls
- softballs
- softball bats
- Hula-Hoops
- jump ropes
- tape player for music

Parents may be willing to donate tennis balls, Frisbees, balloons, beachballs, and other new or used sports equipment. Tennis and racquetball clubs may donate used equipment in good condition. Even major sporting good companies may respond favorably to a letter requesting donations and discounts on new equipment.

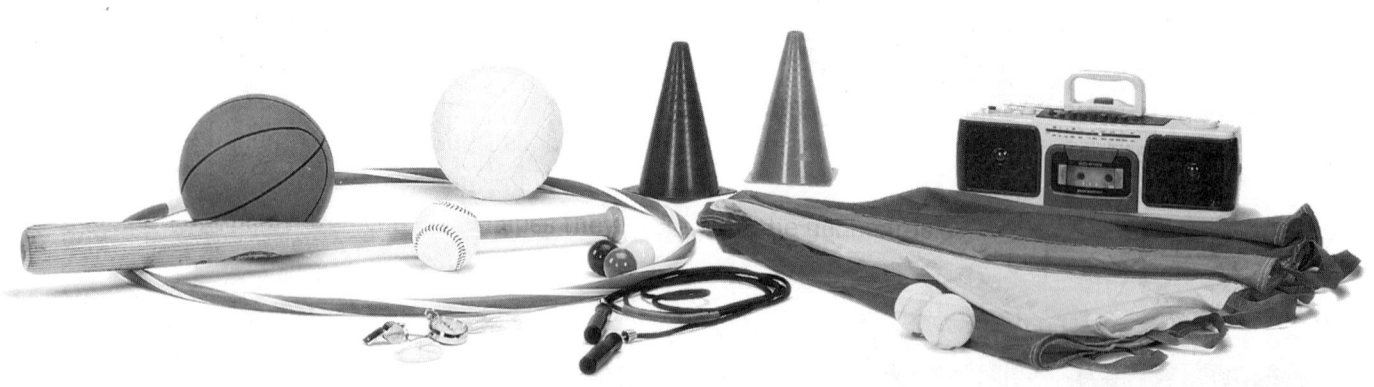

WARMUPS

As an introduction to each lesson, it is important that the students participate in warmup and stretching exercises. These components of the program are important not only for instilling lifetime skills and habits, but also for preserving students' health and safety. It is imperative that students learn to warm up their bodies and stretch their muscles before exercising in order to help prevent injuries.

To accomplish the warmups, the students should line up in their teams and then jog a short distance or perform kick-backs or abdominal crunches according to the directions given below and on the next page.

JOGGING

It is important—and fun—to vary the amount and type of running tasks that the students perform during a lesson. There are many types of jogging exercises that the students can use as an effective warmup at the start of a lesson and as endurance and agility builders during the lesson.

The most basic exercise is jogging a specific distance. The students should jog for a given distance in a specific direction, such as clockwise around the perimeter of the playground. An alternative is to allow the students to jog in any direction at any speed for a given amount of time. For this warmup, the teacher should be sure that there is a clear running area and specific boundaries.

Another jogging alternative is to have the students change the direction in which they are jogging at a specific time. The students should be told to jog in one direction, and then at a whistled signal, they must reverse their direction and run the other way. The teacher may also instruct the students to slow down or speed up when they hear the whistle blow. For example, if they hear one whistle, they will slow down; if they hear two whistles, they will speed up; and if they hear three whistles, they will stop.

Yet another way to vary the jogging task is to add movements to the jogging. The teacher can ask the students to move their arms up and down while they jog, or the students can alternate between jogging and walking, skipping, jumping, hopping, or gliding.

FS-32601 Outdoor Play © Frank Schaffer Publications, Inc.

ABDOMINAL CRUNCHES

Abdominal crunches are a form of sit-ups. They differ from the traditional sit-ups in that, when performed correctly, they cause less stress on the lower back. The students should begin by lying on their backs with their legs bent. Interlocking their hands behind their heads, the students should slowly lift their shoulders up off the ground. The students should raise their shoulders only five or six inches before lowering them to the ground. Raising the shoulders and torso any higher can cause pain or injury to the lower back. The first several times the students perform abdominal crunches, they should "crunch" only five times per session. As they become stronger, they can be encouraged to increase the number of crunch repetitions.

KICK-BACKS

Kick-backs are a fun four-count task. They begin with the students standing up straight with their arms at their sides. On the count of *one*, the students squat down and touch the ground with both hands out in front of their bodies. On the count of *two*, they keep their hands on the ground and kick both feet out behind them. On the count of *three*, they bring their feet directly under their bodies so that they return to a squatting position. On the count of *four*, they stand up, completing one kick-back. The class can perform 5 to 10 kick-backs as a warmup activity. They should perform this exercise in unison, calling out the count of each full kick-back as it is completed.

STRETCHING

After the warmup exercises, the class should perform at least 10 stretches each day covering the major muscles of the body. Each stretch should be held for 10 to 15 seconds while using the correct form. The entire class should perform the stretches in unison. The teacher should model each stretch and perform it with the class. When working with older students, the teacher can select one or two students to lead the class in the daily stretching routine. If the students have been separated into teams, a different team can lead the warmup and stretching activities each day.

SUGGESTED DAILY STRETCHES

Standing Quadriceps Stretch

Stand on one leg with the knee slightly bent. Hold the opposite foot with one hand, and pull the heel toward the buttocks. After 10 seconds, switch legs and repeat on the other side.

Hip Flexor Lunge

Stand with one foot in front of the other, toes pointed forward. Bend the forward knee 90 degrees and extend the rear leg back, lowering the hips toward the ground. After 10 seconds, switch legs and repeat on the other side.

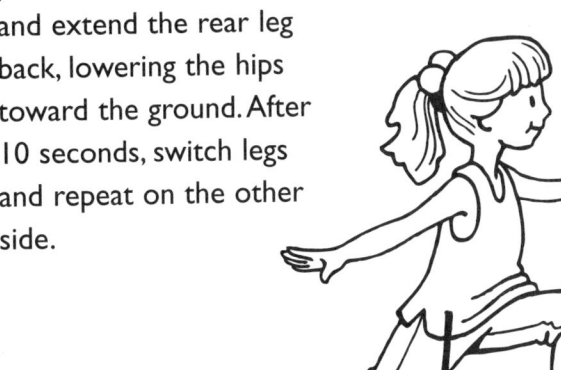

Calf Stretch

Stand with one foot about one foot in distance in front of the other. Keep the heel of the back foot on the ground while leaning the weight forward onto the front foot. Hold for 10 seconds, switch legs, and repeat.

Hamstring Hang

Stand up straight with feet together. Slowly reach down toward the ground with both hands while keeping the legs straight. Reach down as far as possible to feel a comfortable stretch. Hold for 10 seconds.

Crossover Stretch

Stand up straight and cross one leg over the other, keeping the legs straight. Slowly reach down toward the ground with both hands, and let the arms hang for 10 seconds. Slowly stand up, switch legs, and repeat.

Straddle Stretch

Sit on the ground with straight legs spread out as far as comfortably possible. Slowly reach out with both arms toward the left foot and hold the position so that the chest is flat out over the legs in a comfortable position. Hold for 10 seconds and repeat on the right side. Repeat a second time reaching arms straight out in front of the body.

Butterfly

Sit on the ground with feet together and knees bent in the front of the body. The bottoms of the feet should be touching each other. Slowly bend the upper body down toward the feet, while holding onto the feet with both hands. Bend down to a comfortable stretch, and hold it for 10 seconds.

Sit and Twist

Sit on the ground with the legs straight out in front of the body. Take the right leg and cross it over the left leg. Place the right foot on the ground, keeping the knee bent. Slowly turn the body to the right side and place the left elbow on the outside of the right knee. Hold for 10 seconds and repeat on the other side.

Cross Chest

Stand up straight with feet together. Reach the right arm straight across the chest. Place the left hand on the right elbow and pull the right arm into the body. Hold for 10 seconds and repeat with the other arm.

Knee Hug

Lie flat on the ground with the knees bent and feet flat on the ground. Slowly bring the right knee up toward the chest and hold for 10 seconds. Repeat with the left knee. Slowly bring both knees toward the chest, lift up the head toward the knees, and hold for 10 seconds.

Overhead Reach

Stand with feet shoulder-width apart and knees slightly bent. Place the right hand on the right hip and lean to the right. Extend the opposite arm overhead and reach to the right. Hold for 10 seconds. Repeat by leaning to the left side.

Sit and Reach

Sit on the ground with the legs straight out in front of the body. Slowly reach out with both hands and hold on to the ankles, with the chest and head as close to the legs as comfortably possible. Hold for 10 seconds.

Triceps Stretch

Stand up straight with feet shoulder-width apart. Lift one arm overhead with the elbow bent and close to the head. Grasp the elbow with the opposite hand and push down gently. Hold for 10 seconds, switch arms, and repeat.

Arm Circles

Stand up straight with feet just beyond shoulder-width apart. Extend the arms out to the sides, and keep them parallel to the floor. Keep the arms straight and move them slowly to create small clockwise circles. Continue the motion while gradually creating larger circles. Reverse the direction, and beginning with large counterclockwise circles, slowly move to smaller circles. Continue the circles for 30 seconds, changing directions as needed.

Shoulder Rolls

Stand up straight with feet shoulder-width apart and arms straight down at the sides. Slowly raise the shoulders up toward the ears, then rotate them backward and down to the starting position. Repeat four times. Reverse the rotation direction so that the shoulders rotate forward, and complete five repetitions.

Neck Stretches

Stand up straight with feet shoulder-width apart, and place hands on the hips. Keep the chin up, look toward the right, and hold for 10 seconds. Turn the head, look toward the left, and hold for 10 seconds. Repeat turning and looking to each side three times. Next, slowly lower the right ear toward the right shoulder and hold for 10 seconds. Then slowly lower the left ear toward the left shoulder and hold for 10 seconds. Repeat on each side three times.

Seated L

Sit on the floor with one leg straight out in front of the body. Bend the other leg so that the bottom of the foot is touching the inside of the straight leg. Slowly reach out with both hands toward the foot of the straight leg and hold for 10 seconds. Switch legs and repeat on the other side.

Back Stretch

Lie flat on the floor with straight arms extended over the head. Slowly reach as far as possible in opposite directions with the arms and legs. Hold for five seconds, relax, and repeat.

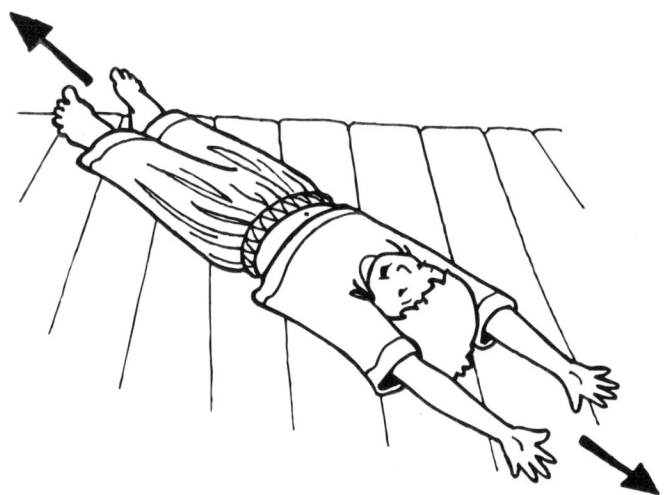

Squat

Stand with the feet shoulder-width apart and the toes pointed slightly out to the sides. Slowly squat down while keeping the feet flat on the ground. Keep the knees to the outside of the shoulders. Hold for 30 seconds.

Cross-leg Stretch

Sit on the floor with the legs crossed over each other. Slowly lean forward and reach out with arms extended as far as possible. Hold in a comfortable position for 10 seconds.

TEAM GAMES

Team games can provide a wonderful experience for all students. Participating in team games helps students develop and refine their physical skills—running, kicking, catching, throwing, and coordination—even as they build their cooperative skills, leadership skills, and good sportsmanship. In addition, students who master the basic rules of a team game can find enjoyment both as a participant in games at school and as a spectator at amateur and professional contests.

Playing team games requires students to work cooperatively to achieve a common goal. Students quickly learn that their team will be most successful when every team member knows the rules of the game and has a basic mastery of the skills required to play the game. Team members learn to help each other master rules and skills. Often, those students who are most skillful can take a leadership role in teaching those who require more practice. Students also learn that playing fairly and showing good sportsmanship make for more enjoyable games.

When introducing students to a team game, be sure to teach and review the game's rules first. Some students may be familiar with most of the official rules, but it is best to establish a common set of rules for use on the school playing field. It is also important to demonstrate the skills required for playing the game and to provide ample skill-practicing time for the students. Plan several practice sessions during which students can work on the rules and skills of the game before they participate in a full game.

For each of the team games in this chapter, you will find descriptions of the game's rules, required skills, and necessary equipment. You will also find a wealth of activities to help students develop and refine their skills. Together, you and your students can discover games that may bring a lifetime of enjoyment to your students.

Kickball

Level of difficulty: moderate

Kickball is a team game similar to baseball that involves catching, throwing, kicking, and running skills. Teams consist of nine players. This game can be easily modified for any grade level by using smaller kickballs and playing fields for younger students.

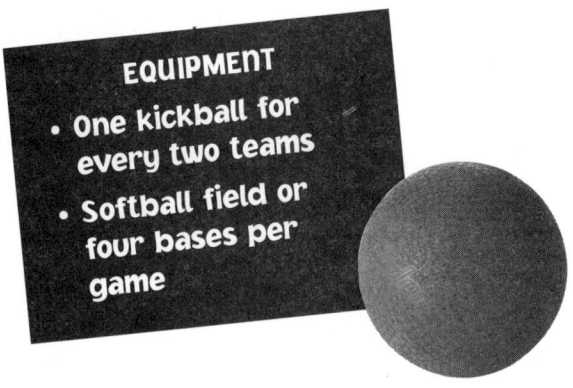

EQUIPMENT
- One kickball for every two teams
- Softball field or four bases per game

GETTING STARTED:

Have students practice kicking, catching, throwing, and running around the bases before engaging in an actual game.

Kicking Skills:

Have the students work in pairs. Have each pair stand 5 to 10 feet apart while kicking the ball back and forth to each other. Have each student practice kicking a ball while it is being rolled, or pitched, to him or her.

Kickball

Catching and Throwing Skills:

Have the students work in pairs. Have each pair stand 5 to 10 feet apart and practice throwing a ball back and forth to each other. Remind the students to extend their dominant arms out toward their partners when throwing and to step toward their targets. Have the partners move farther apart as they become more accurate with their throws.

Have the students practice catching by rolling the ball back and forth to a partner. Instruct them to extend their hands toward the ball and to watch the ball roll into their hands. Then have the partners simulate fly balls by throwing the ball high in the air to each other. Have the partners move farther apart as they become more skilled at catching the ball.

Have the students practice throwing and catching balls from the different positions on the field.

Base-running Skills:

Have each team take a turn running from home plate around the bases and back to home.

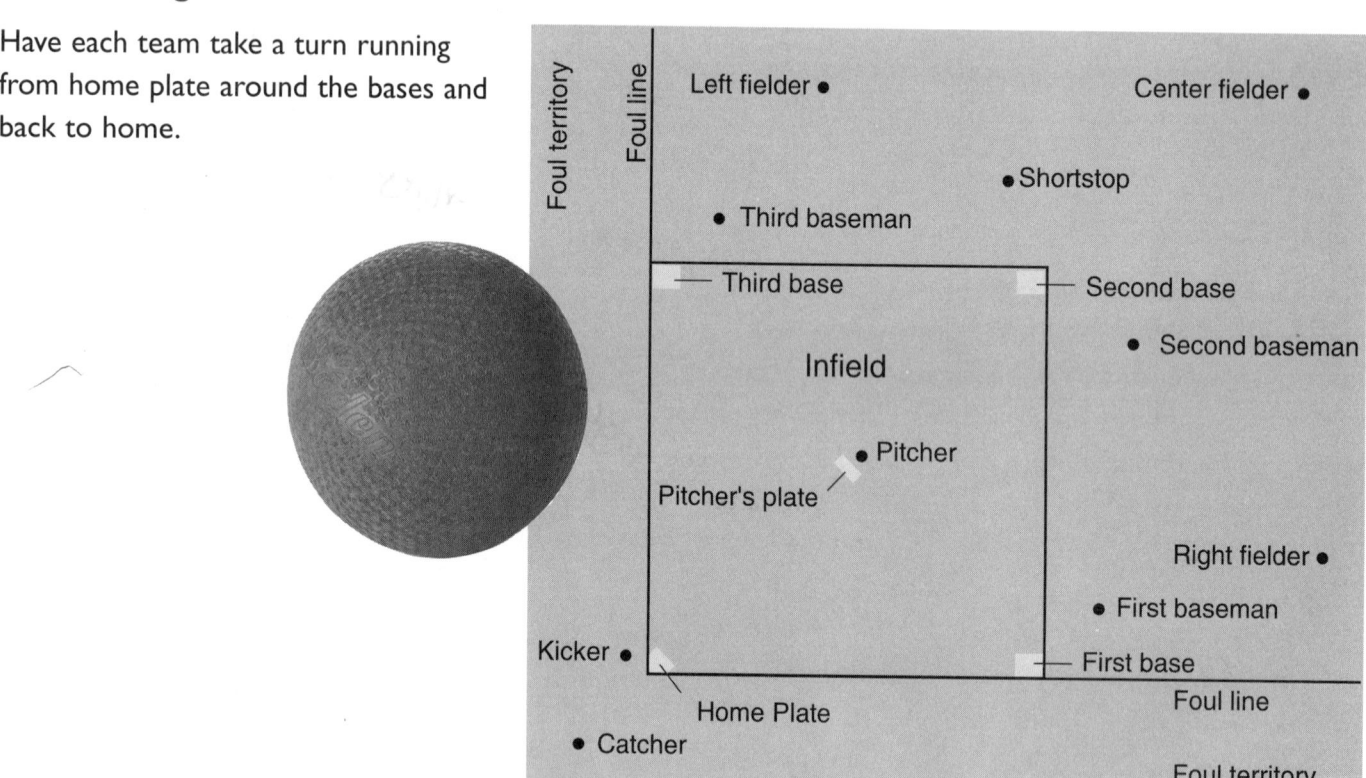

RULES:

There are nine players on a team. A team consists of a first baseman, second baseman, third baseman, right fielder, left fielder, center fielder, shortstop, catcher, and pitcher. To begin the game, one team occupies the field positions and the other team kicks. The pitcher will roll the ball toward home plate and the first kicker. The kicker is allowed three attempts at kicking the ball. A kicker is "out" if he or she misses the ball on three attempts. When a player kicks the ball, he or she must run to first base. The kicker may continue on to other bases if he or she can do so without making an out. The kicker will be called out if the ball is caught before it touches the ground, if he or she is tagged with the ball, or if the ball reaches the base before the kicker gets there. When three kickers on a team are called out, the kicking team occupies the field positions and the fielding team becomes the kicking team. When a runner is safely on base and there is a kicker or another runner behind him or her on the base paths, he or she must run to the next base when a kicked ball hits the ground before being touched by a fielder. If a kicked ball is caught, the runners cannot advance to the next base until after the catch. If there is a vacant base behind the runner, he or she is not required to advance on a kicked ball. A runner must touch each base with a foot and must run directly to each base in a straight line. A run is scored every time a runner reaches home plate.

SAFETY PRECAUTIONS

Players who are not at the plate or fielding a position must be sitting down either inside a dugout or on a bench away from home plate. Do not allow the players to slide into a base.

Basketball

Level of difficulty: challenging

Basketball is a team sport that involves running, throwing, and catching skills. It is played with two teams of five players on a court with a basket at either end.

EQUIPMENT
- One basketball for every two teams
- One basketball court for every two teams

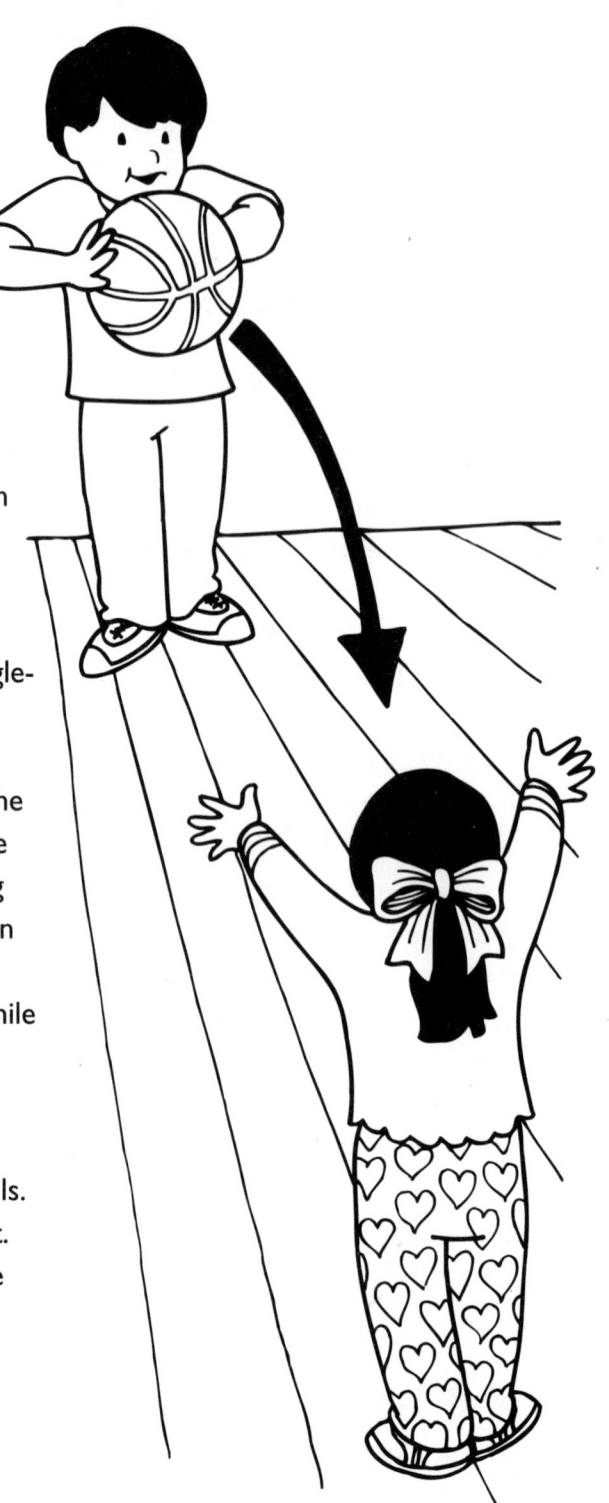

GETTING STARTED:

Have the students practice the following skills before playing an actual game:

Dribbling Skills:

Give one basketball to each team. Have the teams stand in single-file lines along the sideline of a basketball court. Have the first student in each line walk across the basketball court to the opposite sideline while dribbling (bouncing) a basketball with the right hand. When the students reach the opposite sideline, have them turn around and walk back to their teams while dribbling the balls with their left hands. The next person in each line then completes the same exercise. Continue the activity until each student has had a turn. Have the students practice dribbling while jogging and sprinting as well.

Passing Skills:

Have each student work with a partner to practice passing skills. Have the partners stand facing each other about five feet apart. Tell the partners to pass the ball between themselves using the following types of passes:

Chest pass—The student begins by holding the ball with both hands at chest level. The ball is then pushed forward from the chest and released.

Bounce pass—The student begins by holding the ball with both hands at waist level. The ball is then pushed forward and down from the waist and released. It will bounce once on the ground halfway between the two players.

Overhead pass—The student begins by holding the ball with both hands behind the head. The ball is then pushed up and forward before it is released in front of the head.

One-hand pass—The student begins by holding the ball in one hand just above the shoulder. The ball is then pushed forward from the shoulder and released.

Shooting Skills:

Have each team stand in single-file lines behind the free throw line. Give each team a basketball. Demonstrate how to hold the ball properly with the finger tips and the heel of the dominant hand, using the nondominant hand to support the ball. With the ball at shoulder height, push the ball toward the basket with the dominant hand, remembering to follow through—or complete the throwing motion—after the ball is released. Tell the students that a player's shoulders should be squared with the basket and the knees should be slightly bent.

Allow the students to practice shooting first from the free throw line and then from different places on the court. Next, have them practice shooting the ball after it has been passed to them. Finally, let them practice shooting after dribbling down the court.

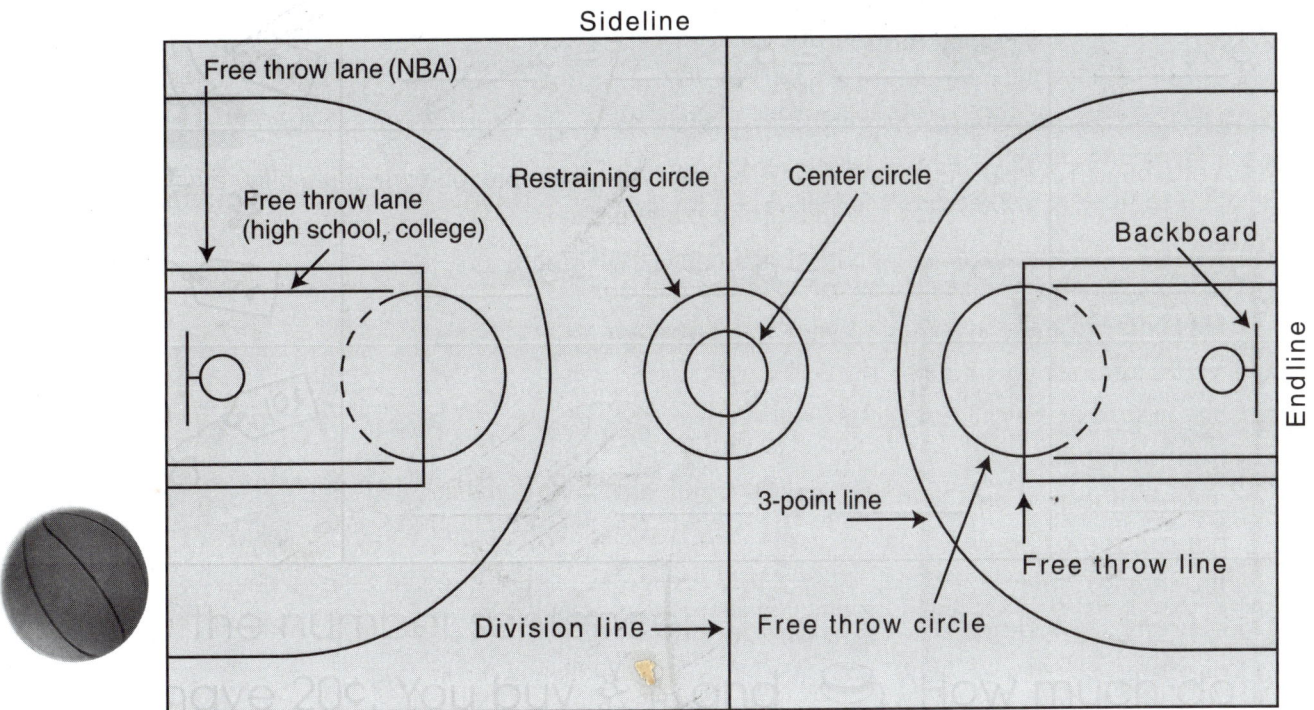

Basketball

RULES:

Each team will defend one basket and will attempt to shoot the ball into the opposite basket. The only ways to advance a ball down the court are to dribble the ball with one hand or to pass the ball to another player. A player may not walk with the ball without dribbling it. Once a player stops dribbling, he or she must either pass or shoot the ball.

If the ball goes out of bounds, the team that did not touch it last will choose a player who will stand outside the court and throw the ball to a teammate. The players may not push, trip, or hit the hand of any other player. When a team scores a basket, it receives two points, and the opposing team will choose a player who will stand outside the court underneath the basket and throw the ball to a teammate.

Since the teacher can only watch one game at a time, physical education basketball requires that the players be on their honor and referee themselves. Before play begins, the players will determine which team starts with the ball by taking turns trying to make a free throw. The first team to make a basket gets the ball. When a player is fouled by an opponent, the teams must agree to let the fouled player shoot a free throw or take the ball out of bounds and resume play. When players on opposing teams tie up the ball (are holding the ball at the same time), the first team to call out "firsts" will retain possession of the ball.

SAFETY PRECAUTIONS

Emphasize the rule that basketball is a noncontact sport. Players may not push, elbow, or slap opposing players.

Flag Football

Level of difficulty: challenging

Flag football is a complicated team game that involves numerous skills such as running, throwing, catching, and kicking. Elementary school flag football is played with teams of six to nine players.

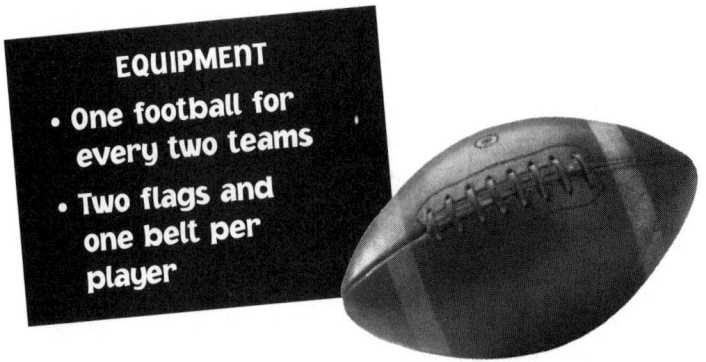

EQUIPMENT
- One football for every two teams
- Two flags and one belt per player

GETTING STARTED:

Students must be familiar with the player positions and skills involved in playing football before engaging in an actual game. To ensure the students' understanding, walk them through a game while explaining each position and the basic rules.

The offense consists of a quarterback, a center, one or two running backs, two or three blockers, and one or two receivers. The center passes the ball between his or her legs to the quarterback, who will either run with the ball or throw it to another player on the team. The running backs stand behind the quarterback. They either receive the ball from the quarterback and then run with it, or they help to protect the quarterback from the defenders. The blockers stand on the line of scrimmage (an imaginary line drawn across the field where the ball is placed) to help the center block the defenders from reaching the quarterback. The receivers line up at the far ends of the scrimmage line and run down the field to try to catch a pass from the quarterback.

Flag Football

The defense consists of three or four pass rushers, one or two pass defenders, and one or two run defenders. The defense must line up facing the offense. When the ball is passed from the center to the quarterback, two or three players will try to rush at the quarterback. Any player may rush the quarterback. The remaining players will defend the receivers or watch the running backs to see if they are handed the ball. The defense should assign players to defend individual offensive players.

After the students become familiar with the basic positions, they should have some time to practice their skills. Throwing the football requires the player to hold the ball with four fingers across the laces and the thumb spread. The student throws the ball by stepping toward a target and snapping his or her wrist as the ball is released out in front of the head. The receiver should catch the ball with two hands in front of the body. When running with the ball, the student should hold it with two hands close to the body in order to protect the ball from defenders. The student performs a punt or drop kick by first taking two steps, then dropping the ball and kicking it with the dominant foot on the third step before the ball touches the ground.

Have each student work with a partner to practice throwing and catching the ball. Then have one partner act as a passer and the other as a receiver. Have the passer throw the ball to the receiver as the receiver runs down the field. Have the partners trade positions after several passes. Finally, have the students practice punting skills by allowing them to kick the balls in an open field. Place several students down field to practice catching the kicked balls.

After the students have had sufficient practice, begin the first games. Have the players line up in the middle of the playing field. Show them the playing field boundaries and goal lines before starting the game. Toss a coin to determine which team will begin the game by kicking off to the opposing team. Usually, the team that wins the coin toss will choose to be on the receiving end of the kick. A kickoff also occurs after a team scores. The scoring team kicks the ball from its side of the field to the opponents' side. The opposing players try to catch the ball and run it back as far as possible before being touched.

RULES:

There should not be more than nine players per team. Absolutely no tackling, tripping, or pushing is allowed. A player carrying the ball will be considered "down" when he or she is touched with two hands below the waist, or when a flag is removed from his or her belt. The offensive team has four opportunities or "downs" to advance the ball a given distance. Blocking is only allowed with the arms crossed and not with the hands.

All players must stay behind the scrimmage line until the ball is snapped to the quarterback. If a player from either team goes "offside" (moves forward before the ball is snapped), the ball will be moved five yards in the direction of the goal line that the penalized team is defending. The team may run with the ball or pass it to any other player on the team except for the center (the person who snaps the ball to the quarterback). The defenders may not push, trip, or tackle the person who is running or trying to catch the ball. If the ball is fumbled to the ground, it is automatically dead and will be awarded at that spot to the last team that touched it. If the defense intercepts a pass, the student who intercepted the ball may run with it until touched. If the offense chooses, on the fourth down it may punt (drop kick) the ball to the opposing team.

When a team crosses the goal line with the ball, it scores six points. The team gets one opportunity for an extra point by starting a play five yards away from the goal line. The extra point may only be earned by crossing the goal line. The scoring team must then kick the ball to the opposing team.

The ball must stay inside the field boundary lines at all times. If a player goes out of bounds, the ball will be played from the point at which the ball crossed the boundary line.

Any infraction of the rules results in a five-yard penalty, which means that the ball will be moved back five yards toward the goal line that the penalized team is defending.

SAFETY PRECAUTIONS

An adult should supervise each game so that students do not become overly aggressive. Strictly enforce the rules at all times.

25

FS-32601 Outdoor Play © Frank Schaffer Publications, Inc.

Soccer

Level of difficulty: challenging

Soccer is a popular team sport involving kicking and running skills. Teams consist of up to 11 players.

EQUIPMENT
- Four cones or two goalposts per game
- Several soccer balls
- Whistle

GETTING STARTED:

Have the students lead up to playing a full game by first working on soccer skills.

Dribbling Skills:

Have the students practice dribbling by giving each student a ball and telling them to move the ball forward with a series of light taps. Tell the players to tap the upper-outside of one foot against the ball every time they take a step forward with the opposite foot. Advise the student to begin by dribbling slowly and to increase their speed as skills improve. When the students have some basic dribbling skills, place cones in a jagged line and ask students to stand in single-file lines and take turns dribbling the ball around each cone.

Throwing Skills:

In soccer, players often throw the ball back into play when it is kicked out of bounds (the boundary is the imaginary line running along the perimeter of the playing field). The player stands with both feet on the ground, holds the ball over his or her head using both hands, and throws the ball into play at a teammate's feet. Demonstrate the overhead throw, then pair up the students and have them practice throwing balls at each other's feet.

Kicking Skills:

Have the students practice passing the ball between two partners. First, demonstrate the difference between passing and shooting the ball. Show the students that to pass the ball, players use the middle-inside of the foot, and they make sure that the kicking leg follows through the kick with an upward motion. To shoot the ball (usually to the goal), players use the top of the foot and, again, they are sure to follow through the kick with an upward motion of the leg. Warn the students not to kick with the tips of their toes, as this can result in injury. Pair up the students, and have them first practice passing the ball to each other, and then practice shooting the ball.

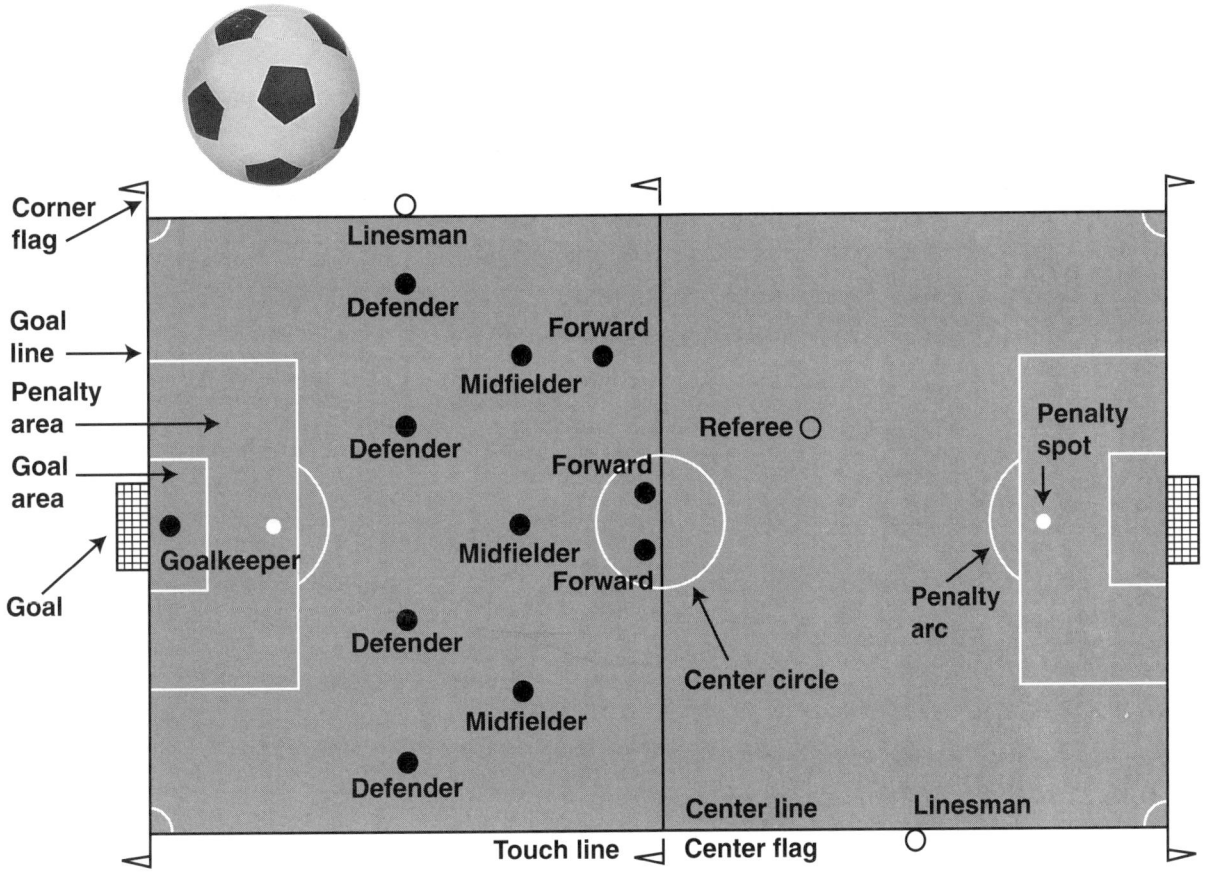

Soccer

RULES:

Each team consists of three forwards, three midfielders, four defenders, and a goalkeeper. The players should spread out over the field according to their positions. The forwards start at midfield and may move anywhere on the field. The midfielders and defenders will stay on their half of the field to defend their goal. The goalkeeper stands in front of the goal to prevent the ball from crossing the goal line. He or she is the only player who may touch the ball with his or her hands. The rest of the players may control the ball only by using their feet to dribble, shoot, or pass. The game begins with the toss of a coin. The team that wins the coin toss may choose whether to kickoff or to defend its goal first. A forward from the offensive team kicks the ball from midfield toward the defensive team's goal line. Whenever the ball is kicked out of bounds, a player on the opposing team must throw the ball back into play, making sure his or her feet do not cross into the playing field during the throw-in. A penalty kick at the goal can be taken by one team when an opposing player kicks the ball out of bounds near the goal. If the goalkeeper ever catches the ball, have him or her throw or kick it back into play from the edge of the penalty area. If the ball ever becomes trapped among a number of players, blow the whistle immediately to stop play.

A goal is scored (one point) when the ball crosses the goal line. After a goal is scored, the team that did not score becomes the offensive team. The teams line up according to their original positions, and a forward from the offense kicks the ball toward the opponent's goal to resume play.

SAFETY PRECAUTIONS

Do not allow the students to kick higher than their waists.

Be sure students understand how to kick safely.

Softball

Level of difficulty: **challenging**

Softball is a team game similar to baseball that involves nine players on a team. Players develop eye-hand coordination and catching, throwing, and running skills. The game can easily be modified for any grade level.

EQUIPMENT
- Several softball bats
- Several softballs
- Several gloves (optional)
- Four bases or a premarked softball field
- Batting tee for younger players

GETTING STARTED:

Have each student practice the following batting, catching, throwing, and running skills before playing a full game.

Batting Skills:

Have each student who is practicing batting stand with feet shoulder-width apart. Have the student hold the bat out in front of the body with the right hand over the left hand (left-handers will have the left hand on top) near the bottom of the bat handle. Have the student practice swinging the bat a few times before tossing a ball to him or her. Direct the student to watch the ball as it flies toward and hits the bat. For younger students, place the ball on a batting tee instead of tossing it to the batter.

FS-32601 Outdoor Play © Frank Schaffer Publications, Inc.

Softball

Throwing and Catching Skills:

Have the students work in pairs. Have each pair stand 5 to 10 feet apart and practice throwing a ball back and forth to each other. Remind the students that they should extend their dominant arms out toward their partners and step toward their targets. Have the partners move farther apart as they become more accurate with their throws.

Have the students roll the ball back and forth to a partner to practice catching. Instruct them to extend their hands toward the ball and to watch the ball roll into their hands. Then have the partners throw the ball high in the air to each other to simulate a fly ball. Have the partners move farther apart as they become more skilled at catching the ball. Have the students practice throwing and catching balls from the different positions on the field.

Base-running Skills:

Have each team take a turn running from home plate around the bases and back to home. Then have each student, one at a time, stand at home plate holding a bat. Instruct the student to swing the bat, drop it on the ground, and run to first base. Make sure that the student understands that he or she may not throw the bat. To emphasize this important safety rule, make it an automatic out if a player throws a bat.

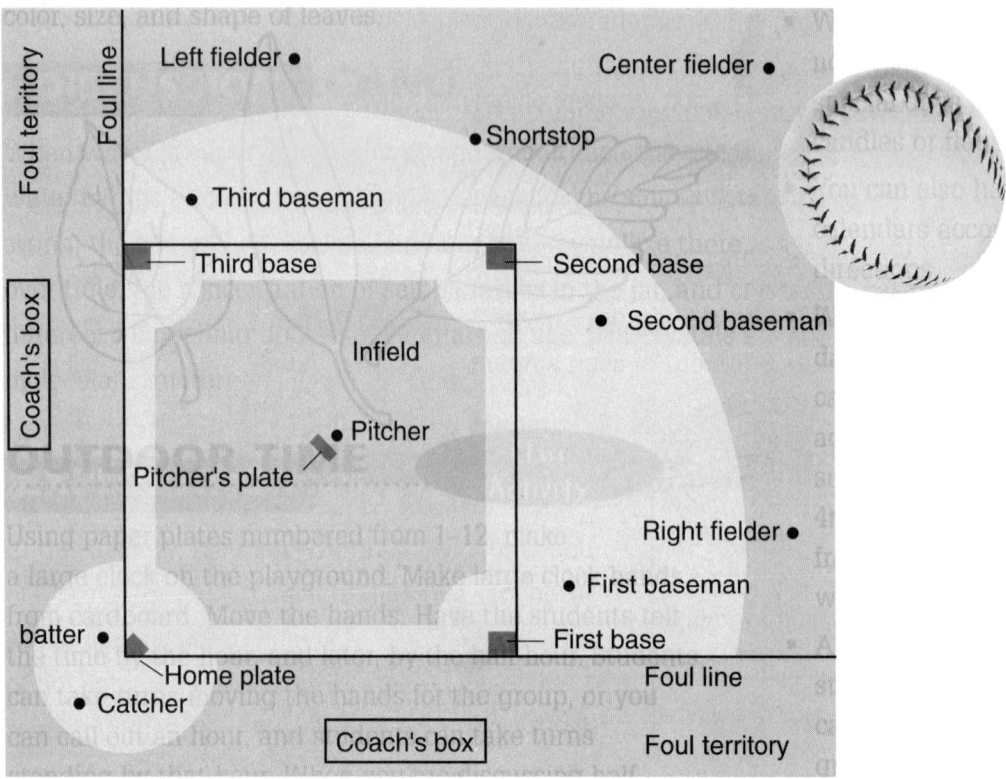

RULES:

Each team consists of a pitcher, catcher, first baseman, second baseman, third baseman, shortstop, left fielder, center fielder, and right fielder. To begin the game, one team will bat and the other team will play the field positions. The pitcher will toss the ball to the first batter. If the ball crosses any part of home plate at a height between the batter's knees and armpits or if the batter swings at the ball and misses, the pitch is a strike. If a batter gets three strikes during a time at bat, he or she is out. If the pitched ball reaches home plate outside of the strike zone and the batter has not swung at the ball, the pitch is called a ball. If a batter gets four balls during an at bat, he or she receives a walk and may go to first base and become a base runner.

Younger students will approach the batting tee rather than waiting for a pitched ball. Each tee-ball batter is allowed three swings at hitting the ball.

When a student hits the ball, he or she must run to first base. The batter will be called out if the ball is caught before it touches the ground, if he or she is tagged with the ball, or if the ball reaches the base before the batter gets there. When a runner is on base and there is a batter or another base runner behind him or her on the base paths, he or she must run to the next base when a batted ball hits the ground before being touched by a fielder. If a batted ball is caught, the runners cannot advance to the next base until after the catch. If there is a vacant base behind the runner, he or she is not required to advance on a batted ball. A runner must touch each base with a foot and must run directly to each base in a straight line. A run is scored every time a runner reaches home plate. After a team has three outs, the teams switch places.

SAFETY PRECAUTIONS

Any player who is not a batter, base runner, or fielder must sit down away from the batting area. Batters may not throw the bat after hitting the ball. Do not allow the players to slide into a base.

Volleyball

Level of difficulty: challenging

Volleyball is a team sport that requires eye-hand coordination as well as teamwork skills. It is played by hitting a ball back and forth over a net. Elementary school volleyball is played with teams of six to nine players.

EQUIPMENT
- Several volleyballs
- Volleyball net
- Cones or premarked volleyball court

GETTING STARTED:

Have the students practice passing, setting, and serving skills before playing a full game.

Passing Skills:

Have the students work in pairs. Have each pair stand five feet apart. Demonstrate the forearm pass for the students. This pass entails holding the arms together with wrists and elbows meeting to create a flat surface with the forearms. Caution the students not to interlock their thumbs, as this can result in injury. Remind the students to keep this flat forearm surface while they bend their knees and square their shoulders toward their partners. Have the students practice the forearm pass by passing the ball back and forth to their partners. One partner should start off by tossing the ball to his or her partner, who should return the ball by pushing it up with the arms held in forearm pass position.

FS-32601 Outdoor Play © Frank Schaffer Publications, Inc.

Setting Skills:

Setting the ball means using a soft, easy pass to raise the ball one or two feet above the net so that a teammate can jump high in the air and spike (or strike down) the ball over the net and into the opposing team's court. Have the students work in pairs with each pair standing five feet apart, to begin setting practice. Demonstrate the hand set for the students; select a student volunteer as ball tosser. As the volunteer tosses the ball to you, hold your hands near your forehead with fingers spread out and hands several inches apart. With the index finger and thumb of each hand, create a loosely formed imaginary triangle. Remember—and remind the students—to bend the knees slightly and square the shoulders toward the partner. Have students practice setting the ball to a partner.

Next, have groups of four or five students form circles. Give each group a ball, and challenge the students to keep it in the air as long as possible using either forearm passes or hand sets. Students should count how many times they contact the ball during each rally.

Serving Skills:

Have the students sit along the side boundary lines of the court. Stand behind one of the end lines, and demonstrate the underhand serve. To accomplish the underhand serve, stand facing the net with feet together. Hold the ball in the left hand out in front of the body. Make a fist with the right hand. Step forward with the left foot while at the same time swinging the right arm back and then forward to strike the ball with the right fist. Caution students not to close the fist around the thumb, as this could cause injury. Repeat the demonstration, reminding left-hand-dominant students to reverse the left and right hand directions. Have the students stand in a single-file line behind an end line. Have each student in turn practice using the underhand serve to strike the ball over the net and into the opposite court.

Next, demonstrate the overhand serve. Hold the ball and toss it in front of the head with the left hand. Hit the ball over the head with the heel of the right hand. Remind the students to face their target and follow through with the serve motion after the ball is struck. Have each student in turn practice using the overhand serve to strike the ball over the net.

For additional practice, place a target on the ground on the opposite side of the court. Challenge the students to serve the ball over the net and try to hit the target.

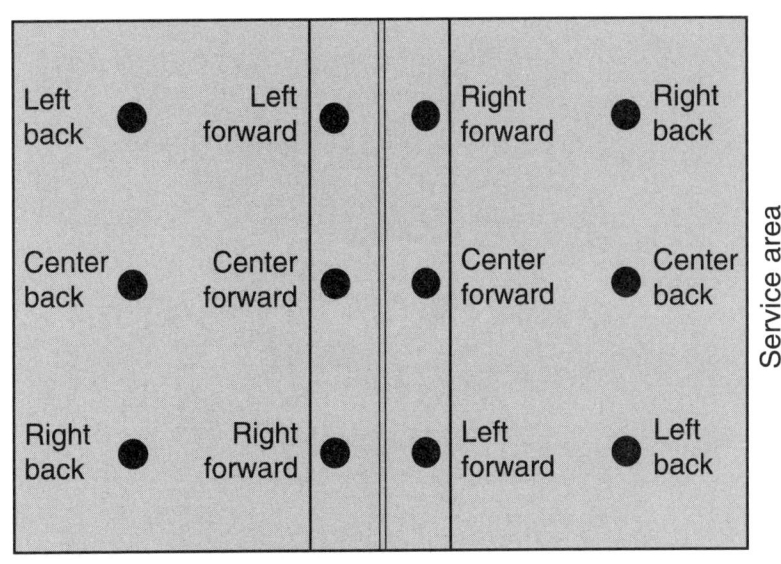

Left back	Left forward			Right forward	Right back
Center back	Center forward			Center forward	Center back
Right back	Right forward			Left forward	Left back

Service area

Net

FS-32601 Outdoor Play © Frank Schaffer Publications, Inc.

Volleyball

RULES:

The two teams stand on opposite sides of the net. One team puts the ball in play by having one player serve the ball over the net from behind the end line. The ball must pass completely over the net and stay within the boundary lines of the opposing team. The receiving team will have three chances to hit the ball back over the net. One player may not touch the ball two times in succession. If the ball is not returned over the net and into play within three hits, the serving team receives a point. If the ball is properly returned, the serving team has three chances to return the ball. If the receiving team returns the ball and the serving team does not successfully return the ball, the receiving team will get the ball and becomes the serving team. This is called a "side out." When a team gets a side out, the players will rotate clockwise around the court. No player may touch the net or cross over the center line of the court. The game ends when a team has earned 15 points.

SAFETY PRECAUTIONS

Be sure that the players are spread out evenly around the court. Do not place more than nine players on a side.

COOPERATIVE GAMES

Cooperative group games and activities are ideal for building cooperation and trust among students. The students must work together in small groups to complete the given tasks for each activity.

The activities are noncompetitive so students of every skill level will feel comfortable participating. The students challenge themselves to perform at increasingly higher levels. They encourage one another and must cooperate, motivate, and respect each other in order to complete each activity. When choosing activities, be sure to pick those that are appropriate for the skill level of your students.

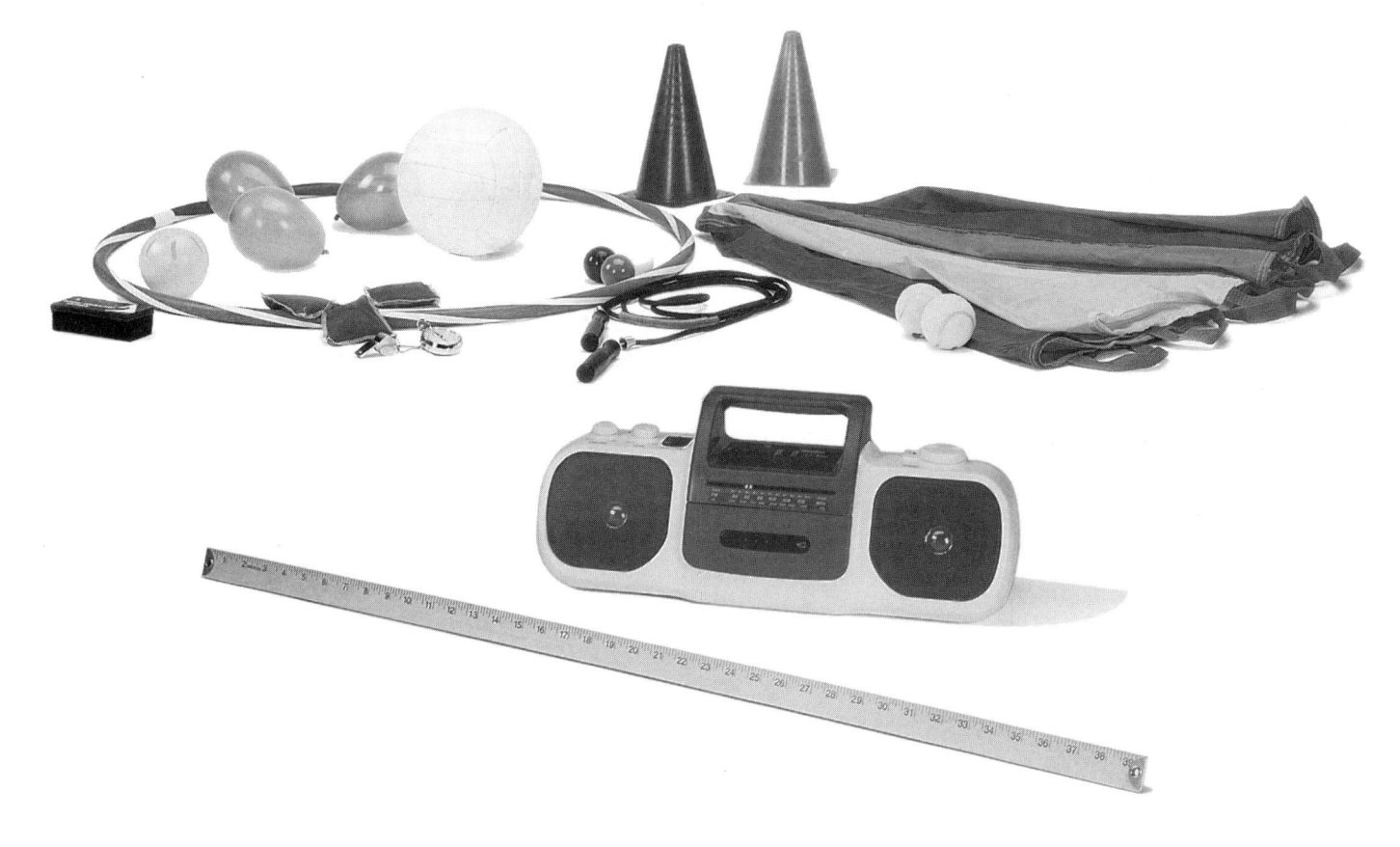

Balloon Dodge Ball

Level of difficulty: simple

Balloon Dodge Ball is a safer alternative to the standard dodge ball game. The activity should be played in groups of six to eight students.

EQUIPMENT
- Several balloons for each group

GETTING STARTED:

Inflate several balloons for each group. Have each group form a circle. Have one player from the group stand inside the circle. Give each group one balloon.

RULES:

The players forming the circle will hit the balloon at the player standing in the middle of the circle. Players may use only their hands to hit the balloon. When the player in the middle is hit by the balloon, he or she must trade places with the player who hit the balloon last. If a balloon is popped, replace it with another one. For a challenge, have each group hit two or three balloons, simultaneously, at the player in the middle of the circle.

SAFETY PRECAUTIONS

Do not allow the students to hold the balloons near their mouths or faces.

Crazy Cones

Level of difficulty: simple

Crazy Cones is a noncompetitive activity for students to practice moving through space while working in two large groups.

EQUIPMENT
- Music or a whistle
- At least one plastic cone per student

GETTING STARTED:

Divide the students into two teams—Team A and Team B. Scatter all of the cones within a large playing area. Half of the cones should be lying down, while the other half is left standing.

RULES:

Instruct the students to listen for the music or a whistle signal. On the signal, Team A will try to knock down all of the cones, while Team B will try to stand up the cones that are lying down. When the music stops (or the whistle blows), the students will freeze. For the next round, have the teams switch tasks and repeat the activity. For subsequent rounds have the students knock down the cones using a different body part such as feet, knees, or elbows.

SAFETY PRECAUTIONS

Emphasize that the students may not run at any time. They must stay within the boundaries and must always freeze when the music stops.

Double Ball Toss

Level of difficulty: simple

This is a ball-tossing game played in groups of three that requires eye-hand coordination and fast reflexes.

EQUIPMENT
- Two small balls per group
- Whistle

GETTING STARTED:

Divide the students into groups of three. Have the groups stand several feet apart from one another. Instruct each group to stand in a triangular arrangement with several feet between each player. Give a ball to each of two students in the group.

RULES:

When the whistle is blown, each group will begin tossing its two balls clockwise around the triangle. No student may have both balls at the same time. If a ball is dropped, it must be picked up and immediately returned to play. When the whistle is blown a second time, the students will reverse the direction in which they toss the balls. Each student should count the number of times he or she can successfully catch a ball without dropping it. Challenge each group to complete a specific amount of successful catches within a given time frame.

SAFETY PRECAUTIONS

Be sure to use balls that are soft. Remind the students not to throw the balls too hard at one another.

Dragon's Tail

Level of difficulty: simple

This is a multicultural game that originated in China. The students form a human dragon with five or six people and play a chase game.

EQUIPMENT
- none needed

GETTING STARTED:

Divide the students into groups of five or six. Instruct the students to line up in their groups. Have each student place his or her hands on the shoulders of the student in front of him or her. Tell the students that each group is going to pretend to be a dragon and that dragons love to chase their tails.

RULES:

The first student in each line is the dragon's head. The last student in each line is the dragon's tail. The remaining students in each line are the dragon's body. The dragon's head must lead the rest of the body around toward the tail until the head can tag the tail. Players must keep their hands on the shoulders of the person in front of them at all times. Allow the groups two or three minutes of chasing and then give a signal to stop. Have the students switch positions and begin again. Repeat until each student has had the opportunity to be both the head and the tail of the dragon.

SAFETY PRECAUTIONS

Allow for plenty of open space for the groups so that they do not run into one another.

Hop Sticks

Level of difficulty: simple

This is a simple game that involves teams of five students. It encourages coordination and pattern development.

EQUIPMENT
- One stick or ruler per player

GETTING STARTED:

Organize the class into groups of five. Give each student a stick or a ruler. Have each group lay out its sticks in a row. The sticks should be about one and a half feet apart.

RULES:

Each group will line up behind its row of sticks. The first player in line must hop on one foot over each stick in the row. Then he or she must pick up the last stick in the row, turn around, hop back over the sticks again, and touch the next player in line. This pattern continues until all of the sticks have been picked up. Players may not touch any of the sticks with their feet. If they touch the ground with both feet or touch a stick, they must return to the starting position and begin again. Repeat the game with the players in different positions in line. For variation, have the groups race against one another to see which group can pick up all of its sticks the quickest.

SAFETY PRECAUTIONS

If you are using sticks, make sure that they do not have any sharp edges.

Jumper Ball

Level of difficulty: simple

Jumper Ball is a noncompetitive game for students to practice trust, listening skills, and coordination. Students work on their jumping skills in groups of 8 to 10.

EQUIPMENT
- One medium-sized ball per group

GETTING STARTED:

Divide the students into groups of 8 to 10. Instruct each group to sit or kneel on the grass in a large circle.

RULES:

One student will be the *jumper* and will stand in the middle of the circle with legs shoulder-width apart. The jumper will close his or her eyes. A student sitting in the circle will roll the ball at the jumper's feet. When the ball is about to hit the jumper's feet, the roller will call out, "Jump!" The jumper will attempt to jump over the ball and then turn and face the student who has caught the ball. Each jumper gets three jumps. Then the last student holding the ball becomes the jumper.

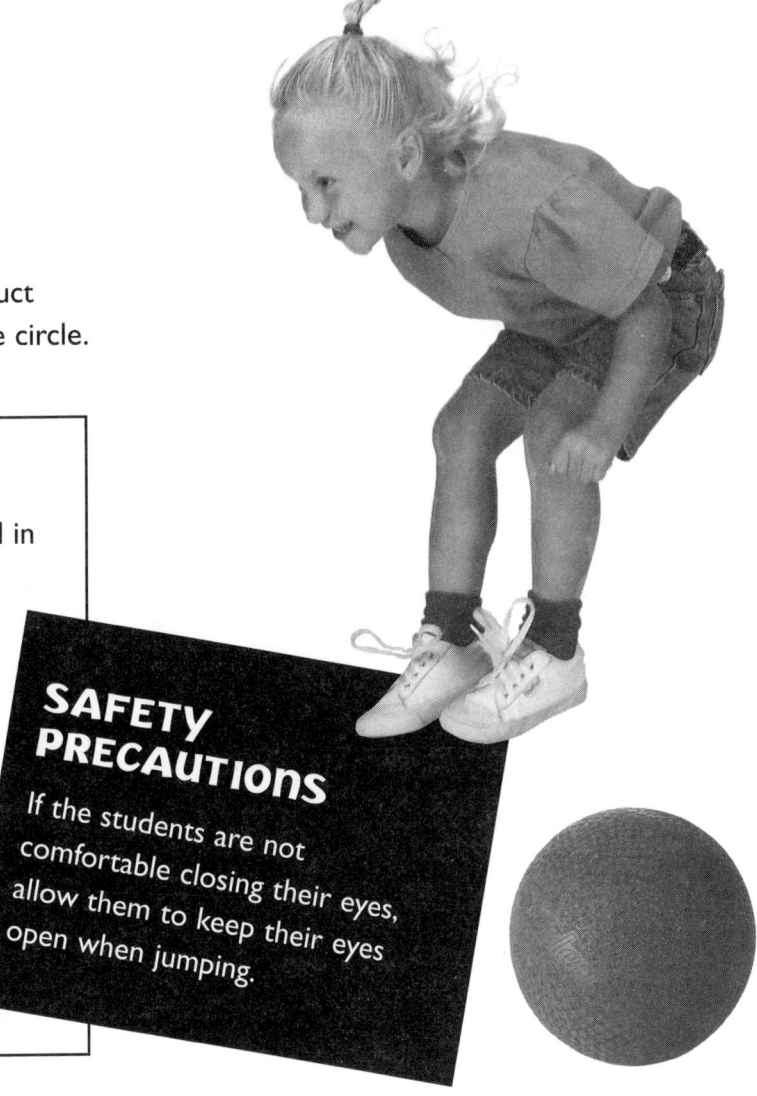

SAFETY PRECAUTIONS

If the students are not comfortable closing their eyes, allow them to keep their eyes open when jumping.

Leapfrog

Level of difficulty: simple

Leapfrog is a simple game requiring jumping and cooperation skills. It is played in groups of 5 to 10 students.

EQUIPMENT
- none needed

GETTING STARTED:

Have groups of 5 to 10 students line up in single-file lines.

RULES:

The first player in each line will squat down and place both hands on his or her knees. The second player will place both hands on the squatter's back and leap over the squatter. The second player will then squat down while the third player leaps over the first two players, one at a time. This pattern continues until everyone has had the opportunity to leap.

SAFETY PRECAUTIONS

Be sure that the students place their hands on the backs of the squatters in order to help propel themselves over.

Man in the Middle

Level of difficulty: simple

This is a simple tag game that can be played with the entire class.

EQUIPMENT
- Basketball court

GETTING STARTED:

Use a basketball court as the playing area for this game. Choose one student to stand in the middle of the playing area. This student is a tagger. Divide the rest of the students into two groups. Have one group stand behind the line at one end of the basketball court and the other group stand behind the opposite line.

RULES:

When the tagger calls out, "Go," all the players must try to run from one boundary line to the opposite boundary line without being tagged. Any student who is tagged will join the tagger in the center and become a tagger. When all of the untagged players reach the boundary lines, begin again. Continue until only one person is left that has not been tagged.

SAFETY PRECAUTIONS

If a basketball court is not available, be sure to create a large area with plastic cones so that there is plenty of running room.

Mirrors

Level of difficulty: simple

This is an aerobic activity for partners that involves moving through space.

EQUIPMENT
- Whistle
- Four plastic cones

GETTING STARTED:

Use two plastic cones to designate a starting line and two cones to designate a finish line. Have each student work with a partner. Instruct each pair of students to line up at the starting line. Assign one person in each pair the task of being the leader.

RULES:

The leader and the partner will jog side by side toward the finish line. The leader will change jogging speeds and directions, and the partner will imitate the leader's actions. When the whistle is blown, the partners will switch roles.

SAFETY PRECAUTIONS

Allow for an adequate amount of running space so that the students do not run into each other.

Pinball Soccer

Level of difficulty: simple

This is an excellent lead-in game for playing soccer. The class plays in teams of five to eight players.

EQUIPMENT
- Several soccer balls per game
- Ten empty milk cartons per game
- Four plastic cones or playground lines per game

GETTING STARTED:

For every two teams, designate a playing area with plastic cones or existing playground lines. Divide the students into teams of five to eight players. Have the teams line up at opposite ends of the playing area. Place the milk cartons in a line midway between the two teams.

RULES:

The players on each team will take turns kicking a ball toward the milk cartons. The kicker must stand behind the boundary line of the playing area. The object is to knock down the milk cartons. When all of the cartons have been knocked down, a designated player from each team will place them upright again before beginning the next round.

SAFETY PRECAUTIONS

Do not allow the students to enter the playing area during the rounds.

Shark and Minnows

Level of difficulty: simple

This is an ideal game for younger students, as it involves imagination, cooperation, and movement through space.

EQUIPMENT
- Four plastic cones or playground lines

GETTING STARTED:

Use plastic cones or playground lines to designate the boundaries of the playing area. Have all of the students line up at one end of the playing area along the boundary line. Choose one student to be the shark, or tagger, and explain that everyone else is a minnow, or runner.

RULES:

When "All clear!" is called out, the minnows will run toward the opposite boundary line of the playing area. When "Shark attack!" is called out, the minnows must try to run back to their starting line before being tagged by the shark. When a minnow is tagged by the shark, he or she becomes a shark and helps tag the remaining minnows. The game continues until all of the minnows have become sharks.

SAFETY PRECAUTIONS

Remind students not to hit or push when tagging.

Steal the Bacon

Level of difficulty: simple

This group game involves two teams. It promotes speed, agility, and listening skills.

EQUIPMENT
- One beanbag

GETTING STARTED:

Divide the students into two equal teams. Have the students in each team sit side by side. The teams should be facing each other and should be approximately 15 feet apart. Assign each student on one team a number. Repeat number assignment for the other team using the same numbers. For younger students, it may be helpful to write each number on an index card and give the cards to the students so that they won't forget their numbers. Place the beanbag halfway between the two teams. Tell the students that the beanbag represents the bacon.

RULES:

To begin the game, call out one of the numbers assigned to the students. The students whose number is called will run toward the "bacon." The student who reaches the bacon first will grab it and run back toward his or her seat. The other student must try to tag the student with the bacon. If the student with the bacon is able to return to his or her seat before being tagged, his or her team earns a point. If the student is tagged before returning to his or her seat, the opposing team earns a point. Play continues until each student's number has been called at least once.

SAFETY PRECAUTIONS

Make sure players do not fight over the beanbag. Have the students play this game while sitting on the grass.

Beach Towel Volleyball

Level of difficulty: moderate

This game serves as a good lead-in to basic volleyball skills and can be played with or without a net. It should be played with four players on each team.

EQUIPMENT
- One beach towel per team
- One volleyball for every two teams

GETTING STARTED:

Divide the students into teams of four, and give each team a beach towel. Have each player hold a corner of his or her towel. Have two teams face each other. Allow the teams to practice using their towels to throw and catch the volleyball.

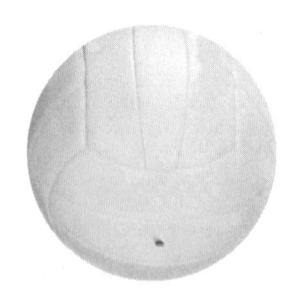

RULES:

Two teams will face each other with a boundary line dividing the teams. One team will use its towel to throw a volleyball to the other team. The other team must catch the ball with its towel and then throw it back to the first team. Play continues until one team fails to catch the ball. The opposing team then earns a point. The first team to earn 15 points wins the game.

SAFETY PRECAUTIONS
Be sure students move in a controlled fashion.

To make the game more difficult, the two teams may stand on opposite sides of an actual volleyball court. The team throwing the ball must get it over the net, and the other team must catch the ball and throw it back. Points are earned when the ball is dropped or does not go over the net.

The next level of play is to put three teams on each side of the court. The game will be played using the basic rules of volleyball. One team on the serving side of the court will serve the ball over the net from behind the back line. One team on the receiving side must catch the ball and pass it to another team on its side before the ball is thrown back over the net. If the teams on the receiving side drop the ball or cannot get it over the net in three tries or less, the serving team earns a point. If the teams on the receiving side successfully throw the ball back over the net and the teams on the serving side drop the ball or cannot return it over the net in at least three tries, then the receiving side becomes the serving side. This continues until one of the sides earns 15 points.

Cars

Level of difficulty: moderate

Cars is a noncompetitive game that encourages students to practice trust and coordination. It should be played in groups of two students.

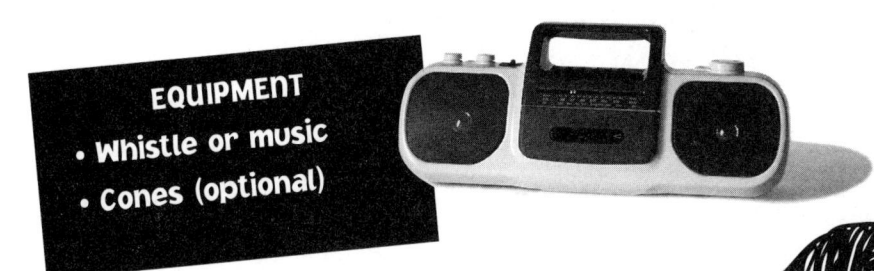

EQUIPMENT
- Whistle or music
- Cones (optional)

GETTING STARTED:

Ask the students how fast they think they would move if they traveled at a rate of one mile per hour. Have the students walk at a slow pace to demonstrate this speed. Then have each student stand facing a partner within a designated playing area. Plastic cones or playground lines can serve as boundary markers. Instruct the students to designate one partner to be the *car* and the other partner to be the *driver*. Have the drivers place their hands on the shoulders of their cars. Explain that the students will take turns at being the car and the driver.

RULES:

On a signal (a whistle blowing or music playing), the partners will travel at the one-mile-per-hour speed limit. The cars will walk backwards as the drivers guide and steer them around the playing area. The drivers may not crash into any other cars, and the cars may not turn around to see where they are going. When the whistle is blown again or the music stops, the cars and drivers must come to a complete stop. Repeat this process for subsequently faster speed limits such as 10 mph, 15 mph, and 20 mph. Students must not travel faster than the designated speed limit. Allow the students to switch roles and partners frequently.

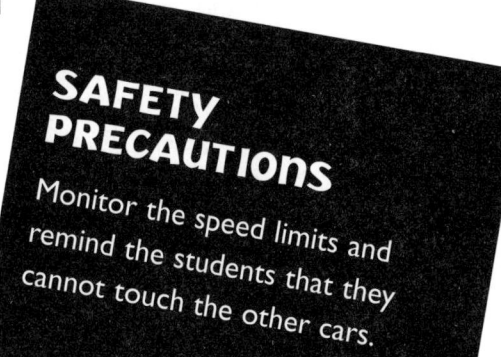

SAFETY PRECAUTIONS

Monitor the speed limits and remind the students that they cannot touch the other cars.

FS-32601 Outdoor Play © Frank Schaffer Publications, Inc.

Crab Soccer

Level of difficulty: moderate

Crab Soccer is an ideal activity for the entire class to play together. It involves four teams of equal size.

EQUIPMENT
- One large rubber ball
- Four plastic cones (optional)
- Index cards (optional)

GETTING STARTED:

Divide the class into four equal teams. Have each team form one side of a square with all of the students facing the middle of the square. Plastic cones may be used to mark the corners of the square. Assign each student on one team a number. Repeat for each of the other teams using the same numbers. For younger students, you may wish to write each number on an index card and give the cards to the students so they won't forget their numbers. Place a ball in the center of the square.

RULES:

To begin the game, call out one of the numbers assigned to the students. The students whose number is called will crab-walk to the center of the square. To crab-walk, the students will place their hands on the ground behind their bodies with their feet on the ground in front of them. To move, the students will walk on their hands and feet. Once the students reach the center of the square, they will each attempt to kick the ball across the goal line of an opposing team. The goal lines consist of the remaining team members who are sitting down forming each side of the square. The students kicking the ball are only allowed to touch the ball with their feet. The students defending the goal lines may touch the ball with any part of their bodies except their hands. If the ball goes over a corner of the square, it should be replayed from the middle of the playing area. When the ball passes over one of the goal lines, a point is scored against that team. Each team must keep track of the number of goals scored against it. After every goal, the players in the center will return to their own goal lines and a new number will be called.

SAFETY PRECAUTIONS

Do not allow more than four players into the middle of the playing area at any time. Do not allow the students to kick the ball above their heads.

Group Juggling

Level of difficulty: moderate

This activity involves groups of eight players. It promotes eye-hand coordination and cooperative group skills.

EQUIPMENT
- Up to five tennis balls, Frisbees, or rubber balls per group

GETTING STARTED:

Divide the students into groups of eight. Have each group form a circle with the players standing about an arm's length apart.

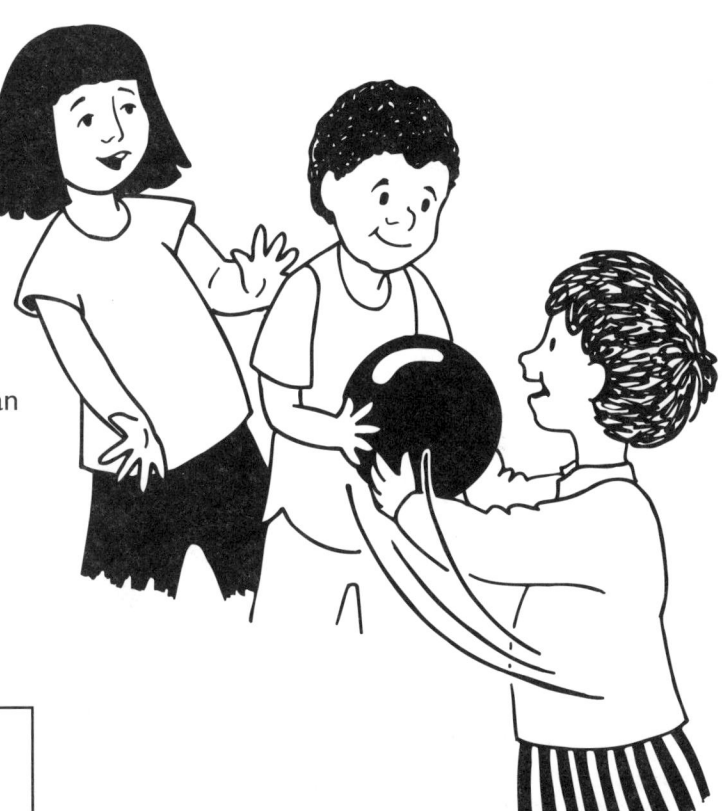

RULES:

To begin the activity, hand one ball to a student in each group. Instruct the group to pass the ball around the circle in a given pattern such as to the left, to the right, or moving back and forth across the circle. Allow each group to practice its own pattern a few times with one ball. Once the pattern is established, add another ball to the circle. Keep adding balls until each group is passing five balls around its circle. Repeat the activity using different types of patterns.

SAFETY PRECAUTIONS

The students should throw the balls at a continuous, moderate pace. Remind the students to stay alert at all times to avoid being hit by a ball.

Long Jump Ropes

Level of difficulty: moderate

This is a cooperative jump rope activity that is most successful when the students work in groups of five or six.

EQUIPMENT
- One long jump rope per group

GETTING STARTED:

Have the students work in groups of five or six. Have the groups stand several feet apart from each other. Distribute one jump rope to each group.

RULES:

Two group members will turn the rope while the rest of the group attempts to jump rope together. The jumpers will run at the turning rope and jump in one at a time until all jumpers are jumping together. The rope turners will trade places with two of the jumpers each time the rope is stopped. Allow each group to create a jumping routine to perform in front of the class.

SAFETY PRECAUTIONS

Provide an adequate amount of space, and remind the students to use care when performing their jumping routines.

One Step

Level of difficulty: moderate

One Step is a cooperative game that develops throwing, catching, and cooperation skills.

EQUIPMENT
- One softball for every two students

GETTING STARTED:

Have each student work with a partner. Have the partners stand about three feet apart facing each other. Give each pair a ball.

RULES:

Each pair of students will throw a ball back and forth to each other. The ball must be thrown in such a way that it can be caught without the catcher moving his or her feet. Each time the ball is successfully caught, the partner who threw the ball will take one step backward. If the catcher moves his or her feet to catch the ball, both partners must return to the original starting line and begin again. The following throws and catches can be used to add variety to the activity: overhand throw, underhand throw, left-hand throw, right-hand throw, two-hand toss, one-hand catch, two-hand catch, and catch after one bounce.

SAFETY PRECAUTIONS

Spread the pairs out so that no one gets hit by a stray ball.

Pickle

Level of difficulty: moderate

This is an ideal lead-in activity for playing softball. It involves throwing, catching, and running.

EQUIPMENT
- Three plastic cones per group
- One softball per group

GETTING STARTED:

Divide the students into groups of nine. For each group, set up three plastic cones in a large triangle. Place one student at each cone as a catcher. Divide the remaining students evenly between the cones. They will be the runners.

RULES:

Each runner will attempt to run between the cones without being tagged by a catcher holding a ball. Runners may not stay at the same cone for more than 10 seconds. They must run directly to another cone or they will be ruled out. The runners will count each cone to which they run without being tagged. The catchers will throw the ball back and forth between themselves. They may not deliberately throw the ball at a runner. Each time the ball is caught, the catcher must try to tag a runner before he or she reaches a cone. The catcher must keep one foot near the cone, and he or she may not chase the runner. If a runner is tagged, he or she must sit in the middle of the triangle until the next round begins. The round ends when all of the runners have been tagged. Challenge the students to surpass their cone total in subsequent rounds. Rotate the runners into the catcher positions.

SAFETY PRECAUTIONS

Runners should not dive at the cones.

Submarine Tag

Level of difficulty: moderate

This is a fast-paced, easy-to-play tag game played by two groups of equal size.

EQUIPMENT
- Four plastic cones or existing playground lines

GETTING STARTED:

Designate a large square playing area with plastic cones or existing playground lines. Divide the students into two equal groups and have the groups stand at opposite ends of the playing area. Choose one student from each group to be a tagger, and instruct the taggers to stand in the center of the playing area.

RULES:

The students will run around the playing area while trying to avoid being tagged. The boundary lines of the playing area are safe zones. The students may enter the safe zones for short resting periods. Students who are tagged must stand on two feet and place their hands on the ground in front of their bodies to create *bridges*. Each student who is tagged must stay in this position until another student crawls under his or her bridge. Then the tagged student may run around the playing area again. When most of the students have been tagged, the game begins again and new taggers are chosen.

SAFETY PRECAUTIONS

Allow the students time between games to catch their breath. Be sure that taggers are not hitting or pushing the other students.

Zigzag Kickball

Level of difficulty: moderate

This cooperative kicking game is a variation of soccer. It is played in teams of five students.

EQUIPMENT
- One soccer ball or kickball per group
- Plastic cones (optional)

GETTING STARTED:

Divide the students into teams of five. Use plastic cones or playground lines to indicate a starting line and a finish line. The lines should be approximately 50 feet apart. Have the members of each team line up side by side at the starting line with one ball.

RULES:

Each team must travel from the starting line to the finish line together. The players must kick the ball from one person to the next down the row until they reach the finish line. Every player on the team must kick the ball. The first team to reach the finish line at the other end of the field successfully will receive a point. The game will continue until each team reaches a predesignated point total.

SAFETY PRECAUTIONS

Be sure that the teams are spread out so that they do not run into one another.

Balloon Volleyball

Level of difficulty: challenging

Balloon Volleyball is an eye-hand coordination game that serves as an excellent lead-in game to volleyball for younger students. It should be played in groups of four students.

EQUIPMENT

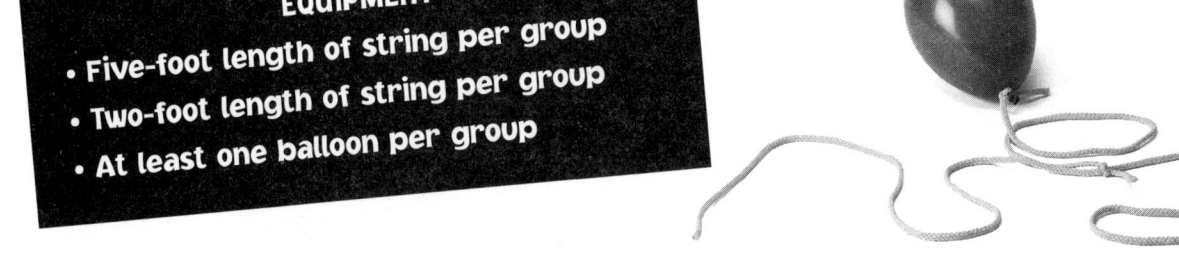

- Five-foot length of string per group
- Two-foot length of string per group
- At least one balloon per group

GETTING STARTED:

Divide the students into groups of four. For each group, tie a two-foot length of string to an inflated balloon. Tie the other end of the string to the center of a five-foot length of string.

RULES:

Each end of the five-foot length of string is held by a student at waist-height. The remaining two players will stand on either side of the string and will bat the balloon back and forth across the string. Instruct the students to hit the balloon with their right hands. After two minutes, have them use only their left hands to hit the balloon. In following rounds, have the students kick the balloon first with their right feet, then with their left feet. Have extra balloons available in case a balloon breaks. Allow the students to switch positions frequently.

SAFETY PRECAUTIONS

Do not allow the students to hold the balloons near their mouths or faces.

Barrel Ball Basketball

Level of difficulty: challenging

This is a perfect lead-in activity to playing regular basketball. Have the students play in teams of four or five players.

EQUIPMENT
- Two equal-sized trash cans per game
- One basketball per game
- Chalk

GETTING STARTED:

Place a trash can, which will serve as a basket, at each end of a designated playing area. For an extra challenge, place each trash can on top of an inverted trash can. Use chalk to mark off an area around each basket. Divide the students into teams of four to five players.

RULES:

Each team will defend one basket and will try to move the ball down the court and throw the ball into the opposing basket. Players may advance the ball only by passing it to their teammates. They may not dribble the ball. When shooting, players must remain outside of the area marked in chalk around the basket. Players must stay within the boundaries of the court at all times. When a goal is scored, the opposing team will get the ball.

SAFETY PRECAUTIONS

Play the game with no more than five players on a team. Do not allow any physical contact between the players.

Blanketball

Level of difficulty: challenging

This activity involves groups of 6 to 10 students using a blanket to bounce balls.

EQUIPMENT
- One full-sized blanket per group
- Several balls of varying sizes per group

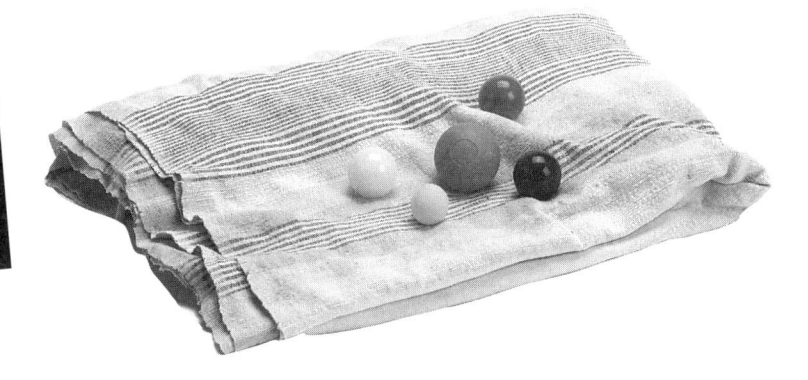

GETTING STARTED:

Give each group a blanket. Have the students spread out evenly around the outer edges as they hold on to the blanket.

RULES:

Place one ball on the blanket, and instruct the students to shake the blanket so that the ball goes up in the air. Assign one student to be the ball retriever for each group. Have each group experiment with tossing the ball to different heights without allowing the ball to hit the ground. Next, place several more balls on each group's blanket, and challenge the groups to toss the balls into the air with the blankets. Have them try to catch as many balls as possible. When all of the balls have fallen to the ground, send the retrievers after them. The game becomes challenging as more balls are added to the blanket. Time the groups to see which group can keep the balls in the air for the longest time.

SAFETY PRECAUTIONS

Keep the groups spread apart so that they do not interfere with one another. Allow only one student per group to retrieve the stray balls.

Crows and Cranes

Level of difficulty: challenging

Crows and Cranes is a group tag game that has no winners or losers. It involves two equal teams and can be played with almost any age group.

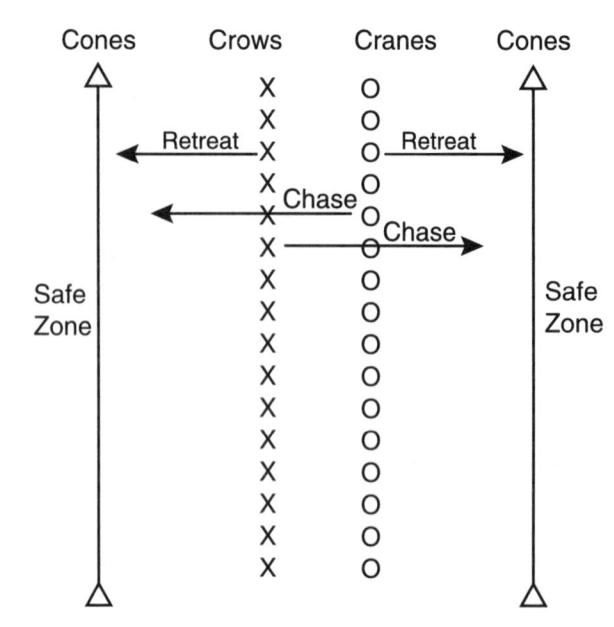

EQUIPMENT
- Lines on the playground or six plastic cones

```
        Cones   Crows   Cranes   Cones
          △       X       O        △
                  X       O
              ←Retreat X   O  Retreat→
                  X       O
                  X   Chase O
              ←   X       O Chase →
                  X       O
        Safe      X       O      Safe
        Zone      X       O      Zone
                  X       O
                  X       O
                  X       O
                  X       O
                  X       O
                  X       O
                  X       O
          △                        △
```

GETTING STARTED:

Use existing playground lines or plastic cones to designate two goal lines that are about 50 feet apart. In the center of the playing area, designate two starting lines that are about three feet apart. Divide the students into two equal teams. Name one team *Crows* and the other team *Cranes*. Have the *Crows* stand on one starting line and the *Cranes* on the opposite starting line. The students should be facing each other. The goal line behind each team is that team's safe zone.

RULES:

To begin each round, call out one team's name, and that team will chase the other team back into its safe zone. If a player on the chasing team can tag an opposing player before he or she reaches the safe zone, the tagged player will become a member of the chasing team. If a player reaches the safe zone, he or she can not be tagged. After each round, all players return to the starting lines and the teacher will call out another name. No score is kept.

Test how carefully the students are listening by calling out words that rhyme with *crows* and *cranes* such as *toes*, *rows*, *planes*, or *trains*. Students who begin to run when rhyming words are called instead of team names will change teams.

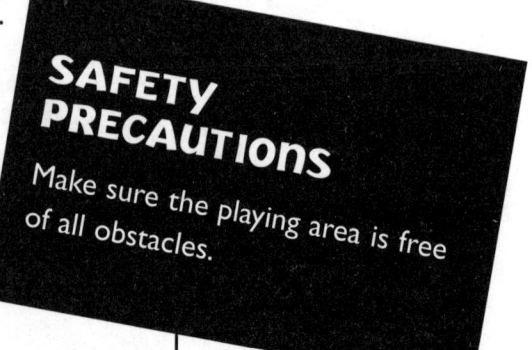

SAFETY PRECAUTIONS
Make sure the playing area is free of all obstacles.

Grass Drills

Level of difficulty: challenging

This activity builds the students' running endurance and upper-body strength. It also promotes cooperative group skills.

EQUIPMENT
- Four plastic cones
- Whistle

GETTING STARTED:

Use plastic cones to designate a large rectangular playing area on a grass field. Divide the students into teams of three. Have the teams stand several feet apart from each other in single-file lines around the perimeter of the playing area.

RULES:

When the whistle is blown, each team will jog around the playing area in a single-file line. Students must jog at a continuous, moderate pace. When the whistle is blown again, the student at the end of each line will drop to the ground and perform a push-up. During this time, the other members of the team will continue jogging. After completing the push-up, the student must stand up and run to the front of his or her line. At the next whistle, the last student in line will drop and perform a push-up while the others continue jogging. The activity continues until every member of the team has had several chances to perform push-ups.

SAFETY PRECAUTIONS

Designate a large enough area for the students to run in without running into other students. Warn the students that they must be careful when they drop to the ground.

Ultimate Handball

Level of difficulty: challenging

This team game is a lead-in to playing soccer or football. It involves throwing and catching skills and should be played with two equal teams.

EQUIPMENT
- Eight plastic cones
- One small or medium-sized ball

GETTING STARTED:

Place a plastic cone at each corner of a large playing field to indicate the boundaries for the game. Create goal markers by placing two cones about 10 feet apart in the center of the boundary lines on opposing sides of the field. Divide the students into two equal teams.

RULES:

The object of the game is for each team to try to move the ball down the field and throw it through the opposing team's goal to score a point. The players may not run with the ball. To move the ball, a player must throw it to a teammate. Players on the opposite team may try to intercept the ball or knock it away from the player trying to catch it. Once the ball has been caught, all players must move approximately three feet away from the player holding the ball. That player has five seconds to throw the ball to another teammate, or the ball is forfeited to the other team. When a goal is scored, the team that did not score will select a player to throw the ball in from the goal line.

SAFETY PRECAUTIONS

Be sure to have clear sideline boundaries. Enforce the three-feet defense rule to avoid contact between players.

RELAYS

Relay activities involve groups of five to eight students. Relays require the students to work together to complete a task. Each group member must perform the exact same task one at a time. A relay is completed when each group member has completed the assigned task.

Relays are unique in that they involve individual participation in a group setting. Students must be supportive of one another in a team atmosphere. Relays generate excitement by challenging the students to perform to the best of their abilities. The students encourage and cheer for one another.

There are no winners or losers in cooperative relays. Every group must complete each given task in order to end a relay. It is not necessary to single out a team for finishing the task first. It is more important to acknowledge effort among the individual teams.

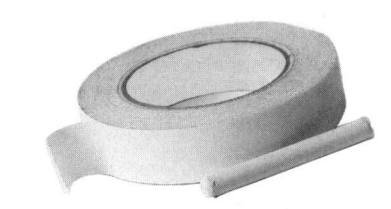

FS-32601 Outdoor Play © Frank Schaffer Publications, Inc.

63

Animal Relays

Level of difficulty: simple

This is an excellent activity for younger students, who complete the relay by imitating the movements of animals. This relay works best when the students are divided into groups of four or five.

EQUIPMENT
- none needed

GETTING STARTED:

Select or mark two lines approximately 20 feet apart to serve as starting and finish lines. Divide the students into groups of four or five. Instruct each group to sit in a single-file line behind the designated starting line on the playground. Explain to the students that in this relay they will be imitating the movements of animals. The diagrams on the next page show suggested movements for a crab, elephant, frog, gorilla, and kangaroo. Demonstrate the desired movement before allowing the students to begin each round of the relay. For example, if the students are to imitate a crab, show them how to place their hands on the ground behind their bodies with their feet on the ground in front of them. To move, the students will walk backwards on their hands and feet.

RULES:

Call out the name of the animal that is to be imitated and illustrate the movement to use in the relay. The first student in each line will move from the starting line to the finish line and back to the starting line in the same way that was demonstrated. When the students return to the starting line, they will go to the ends of their lines and the next student in each line will perform the same task. After each student has performed the task, assign a new animal to imitate. Challenge the students to create the movements themselves rather than modeling specific movements.

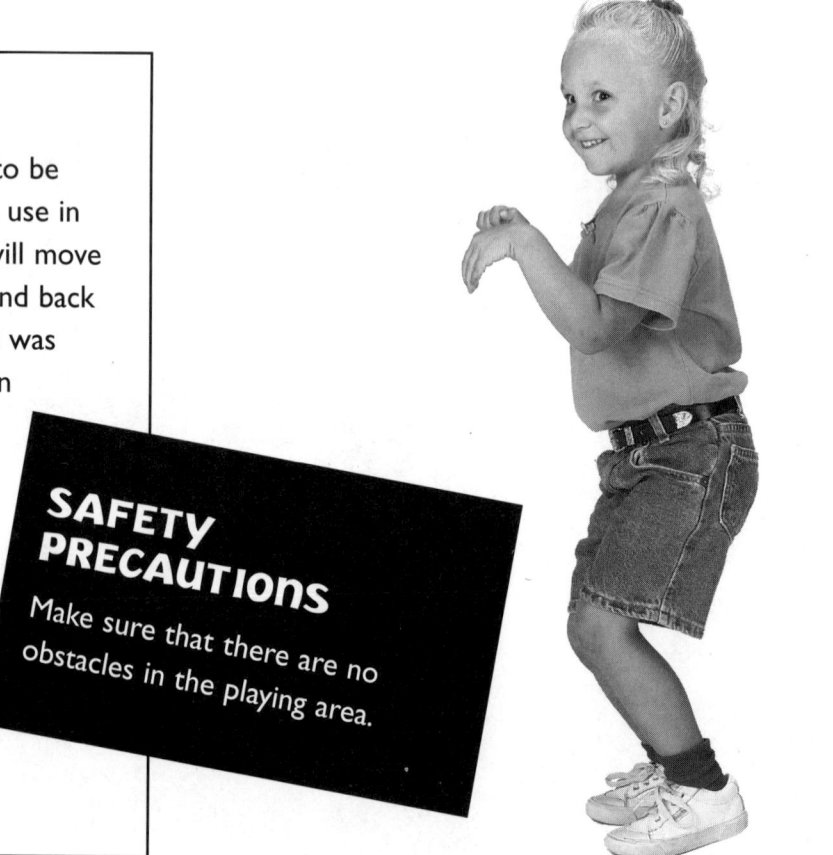

SAFETY PRECAUTIONS
Make sure that there are no obstacles in the playing area.

Crab Walk

Kangaroo Walk

Elephant Walk

Gorilla Walk

Frog Hop

Around the Bases Relay

Level of difficulty: simple

This relay serves as a good lead-in to playing softball, as it focuses on learning how to run the bases on a softball field. The students will complete the relay in groups of seven or eight.

EQUIPMENT
- Four bases or cones

GETTING STARTED:

Use either the existing bases on a softball field or set up bases or cones in a large square. Divide the students into groups of seven or eight. Only two groups will participate at a time. Have the two participating groups line up so that they form diagonal lines directly in front of opposite bases on the inside of the diamond.

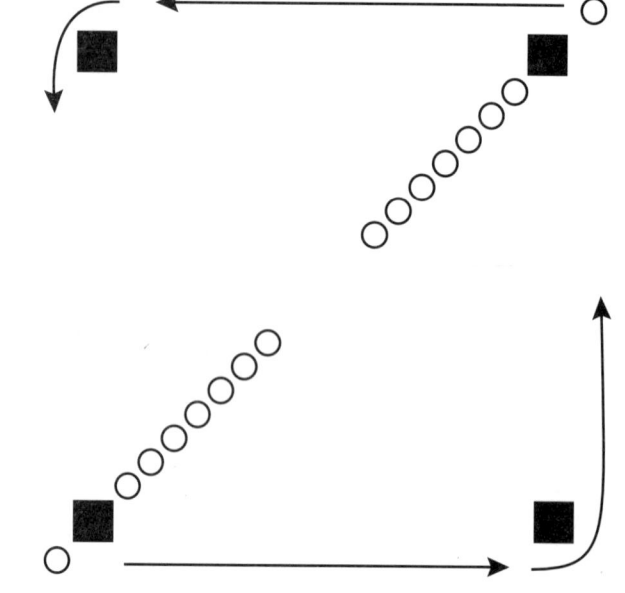

RULES:

The first player in line from each group will run one lap around the four bases and then go to the end of his or her line. The next person in each line will then run the bases. This will continue until each student has completed one lap around the bases. All students must run in the same direction. They must touch each base as they pass it, and they may not interfere with one another.

SAFETY PRECAUTIONS

Be sure to have the groups stand at opposite bases. Strictly enforce the no interference rule.

Hula-Hoop Relay

Level of difficulty: simple

In this relay, Hula-Hoops are used as collection areas for a variety of items. Groups of five students work together to move the items from one hoop to another.

EQUIPMENT
- Two Hula-Hoops for each group
- A variety of items for each group Suggested items: balls, jump ropes, books, erasers, etc.

GETTING STARTED:

Divide the students into groups of five. Have each group stand single file behind the starting line. Place a Hula-Hoop in front of each group about three feet away from the starting line. Place each group's items inside of the hoop. Place another hoop approximately 20 feet away from the first hoop.

RULES:

The first student in each line will run to the first hoop, pick up all of the items within it, and run and place the items inside of the far hoop. The student will then run back to the starting line and tag the next student in line. The second student will run to the far hoop, gather all of the items within it, and return them to the first hoop. The relay will continue until each person on the team has moved the items from one hoop to the other.

SAFETY PRECAUTIONS

Be sure there are no sharp objects among the items to be moved. The students should not throw the items from one hoop to the next.

Change Leaders

Level of difficulty: moderate

This activity requires groups of four or five students to use cooperation, listening, and movement skills.

EQUIPMENT
- Whistle

GETTING STARTED:

Divide the students into groups of four or five. Have each group line up single file at a designated starting point.

RULES:

Each group will move in its single-file line around the playing area. The line leader of each group will choose a movement such as hopping, jogging, skipping, or jumping. All members of the group must perform the chosen skill until they hear the whistle blow. When the whistle is blown, each line leader will go to the end of his or her line, and the new line leader will choose the next skill. This activity continues until every student has had a chance to be the line leader.

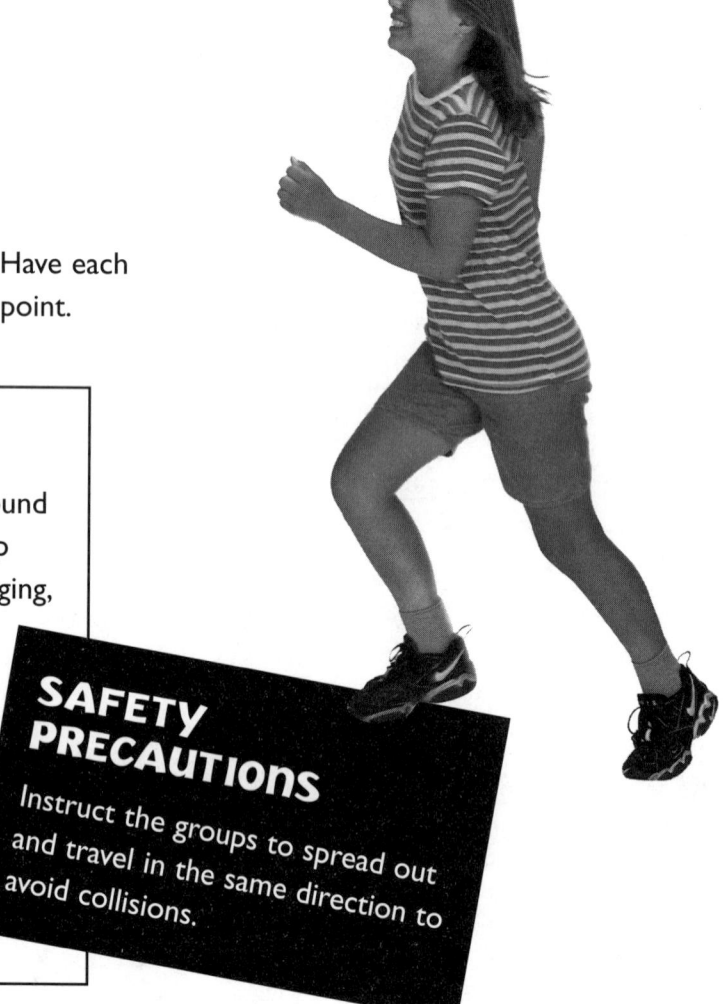

SAFETY PRECAUTIONS

Instruct the groups to spread out and travel in the same direction to avoid collisions.

Continuous Passing Relay

Level of difficulty: moderate

This relay is a good warm-up activity for playing basketball. It involves groups of five players who will practice their ball-passing skills.

EQUIPMENT
- One medium-sized ball per group

GETTING STARTED:

Divide the students into groups of five. Have the members of each group stand in a line side by side. Spread the groups out so that they are a few feet apart from each other. Select one person from each group to be the leader. Give each leader a ball.

SAFETY PRECAUTIONS
Remind the students to pay attention and know when the ball will be passed to them so that it does not hit them.

RULES:

The leader will stand several feet away from his or her group. Then the leader will pass the ball to the student at one end of the row, who will then pass the ball back to the leader. The ball will then be passed to the next student in the row, who will pass the ball back to the leader. This pattern will continue until the last student in the row has passed the ball to the leader. The first person in the row will then face the group and become the leader. The original leader will go to the end of the row. The relay continues until each person has been the leader at least once.

The following types of passes may be used:

Chest pass—The student will hold the ball with both hands at chest level. The ball is pushed forward from the chest and released.

Bounce pass—The student will hold the ball with both hands at waist level. The ball is pushed forward and down from the waist and released. It will bounce on the ground once halfway between the two players.

Overhead pass—The student will hold the ball with both hands behind the head. The ball is pushed up and forward before it is released in front of the head.

One-hand pass—The student will hold the ball in one hand just above the shoulder. The ball is pushed forward from the shoulder and released.

FS-32601 Outdoor Play © Frank Schaffer Publications, Inc.

Dribble Relay

Level of difficulty: moderate

This activity, which reinforces eye-hand coordination, allows students to practice dribbling. This makes it an excellent lead-in activity to basketball. It should be played in groups of five students.

EQUIPMENT
- One basketball per group
- One plastic cone per group

GETTING STARTED:

Divide the students into groups of five. Have each group line up single file behind a designated starting line. For each group, place a cone 15 to 20 feet away from the starting line. Give the basketball to the first student in each line.

RULES:

The first student in each line will dribble the ball with his or her right hand while moving down the playing area to the group's cone. When the student reaches the cone, he or she will continue to dribble the ball while circling the cone and returning to the group's starting line. When the student reaches the starting line, he or she will hand the ball to the next student in line and then run to the end of the line. The relay continues until each group member has completed the course.

This relay can be played using several variations including dribbling with the left hand, dribbling with alternating hands, dribbling while walking backwards, and dribbling around obstacles.

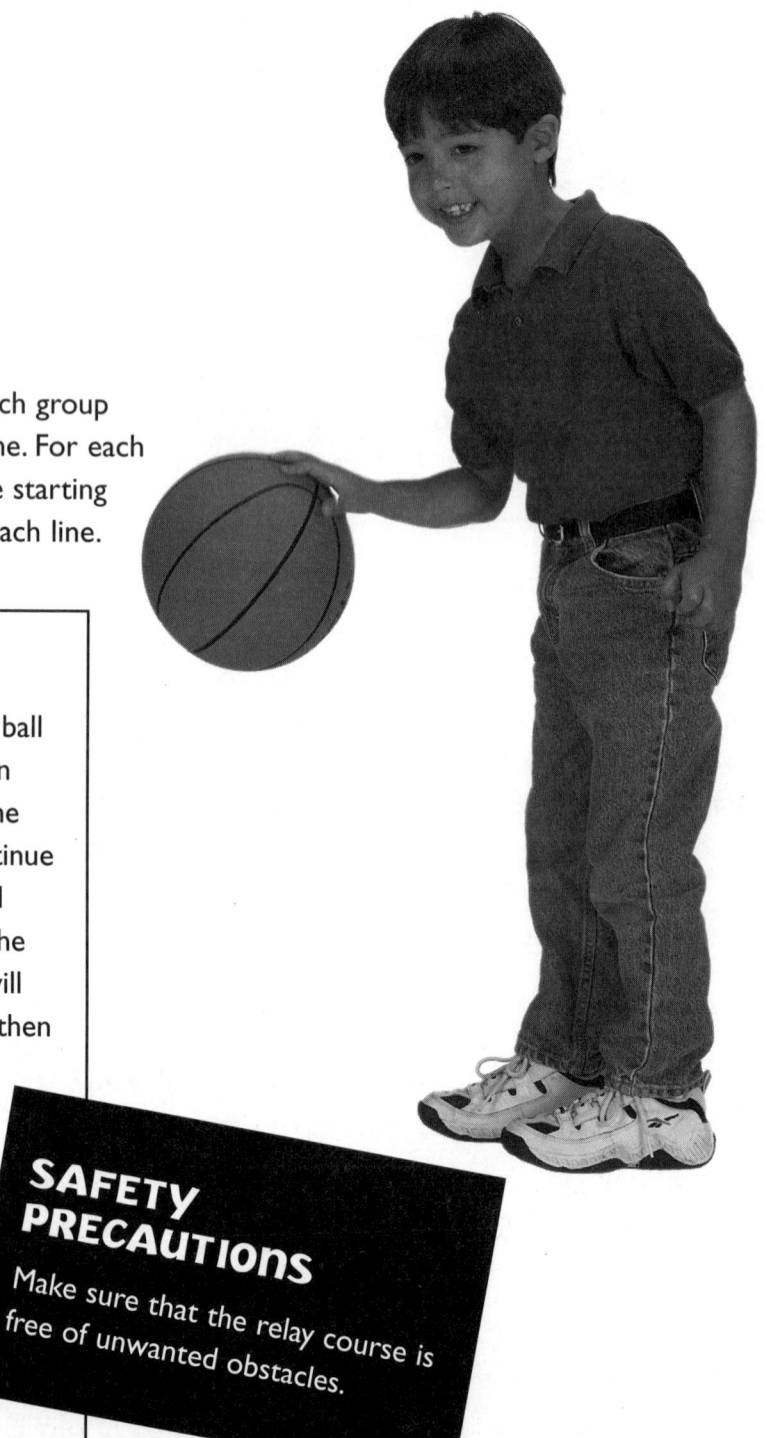

SAFETY PRECAUTIONS

Make sure that the relay course is free of unwanted obstacles.

Kangaroo Relay

Level of difficulty: moderate

This relay requires coordination and balance. Students participate in teams of four to eight players.

EQUIPMENT
- One medium-sized ball per group
- One plastic cone per group

GETTING STARTED:

Divide the students into groups of four to eight players. Have each group line up single file behind a designated starting line. For each group, place a cone several feet away from the starting line. Give the first student in each line a ball.

RULES:

The first student in each line will hold the ball between his or her knees. The student must jump across the playing area while keeping the ball between the knees. When the student reaches the group's cone, he or she will continue to jump while circling the cone and returning to the starting line. When the student reaches the starting line, he or she will hand the ball to the next player in line and then walk to the end of the line. The relay will continue until each player completes the course.

SAFETY PRECAUTIONS

Be sure that there are no obstacles on the relay course.

Long-distance Relay

Level of difficulty: moderate

This relay helps to build endurance by having the students run long distances as part of a six-person team.

EQUIPMENT
- One baton or chalkboard eraser per team

GETTING STARTED:

Divide the students into teams of six. Have each team line up at one end of the field or playground. Give the first student in each line a baton or an eraser.

RULES:

The first student in each line will carry the baton and run all the way across the field. When the student reaches the opposite end of the field or another designated point, he or she will return to the starting line and hand off the baton to the next student in line. The relay is complete when each student on the team has completed the course.

SAFETY PRECAUTIONS

Vary the distance of the running area according to the students' skill levels.

Over-Under

Level of difficulty: moderate

Over-Under requires cooperation and teamwork as students pass a ball in a specific pattern. The relay is most effective when played in teams of 8 to 10 players.

EQUIPMENT
- One medium-sized ball per group

GETTING STARTED:

Divide the students into teams. Have each team stand in a single-file line. Give the first student in each line a ball.

RULES:

The first student in each line will pass the ball over his or her head to the second student in line. The second student will in turn pass the ball backwards between his or her legs to the third person. The third student will pass the ball over the head to the fourth student, who will then pass it backwards between his or her legs. The ball will continue to be passed in this pattern until it reaches the end of the line. The last student in line must take the ball and run to the front of the line and start the pattern over again. The relay ends when the original first student returns to the front of the line with the ball. Anytime the ball is dropped or passed in the wrong manner, the pattern must start over from the front of the line.

SAFETY PRECAUTIONS

Spread the lines apart so that players do not run into each other when running to the fronts of the lines.

Pony Express Relay

Level of difficulty: moderate

This is a long-distance running relay. It is played in groups of six students.

EQUIPMENT
- One baton or chalkboard eraser for each team
- Six plastic cones

GETTING STARTED:

Arrange six cones in a circle with about 15 feet between each cone. Number the cones from one to six. Divide the students into teams of six, and assign each team member a number from one to six. Make sure each student knows who is on his or her team. Then have all of the students who were assigned the *number one* stand by the *number one* cone. The *number two* students will stand by the *number two* cone and so on until each team has one member at each cone. Give each student at the *number one* cone a baton or chalkboard eraser.

RULES:

Each student at the *number one* cone will run to the *number two* cone and hand the baton or eraser to his or her teammate. The *number one* student will remain at the *number two* cone, and the *number two* student will run to the *number three* cone. The baton will be passed to the *number three* student, and the *number two* student will remain at the *number three* cone. The relay continues until each student has returned to his or her starting position.

SAFETY PRECAUTIONS
Be sure that the boundaries of the field are clearly marked and that there are no holes or obstacles along the running route.

Suitcase Relay

Level of difficulty: moderate

Suitcase Relay is a fun game that involves teams of four to six students.

EQUIPMENT
- One plastic cone for each group
- One suitcase packed with adult-sized clothing for each group (suggested clothing: shirt, pants, belt, socks, and shoes)

GETTING STARTED:

Divide the students into teams of four to six players. For each team, fill a suitcase with adult-sized clothing. Make sure each suitcase has the same amount and type of clothing. Have each team line up single file at a designated starting line. Place a suitcase in front of each team about five feet away from the starting line. Place a cone about 20 feet away from each suitcase.

RULES:

The first person in each line will run to the suitcase directly in front of his or her team. The student will put on each article of clothing in the suitcase over his or her own clothes. Then the student will run to the team's cone, circle the cone, and return to the suitcase. When the student reaches the suitcase, he or she will remove all the adult-sized clothing, place it in the suitcase, and run to the end of the team's line. The relay will continue until each player has completed the same process.

SAFETY PRECAUTIONS
Make sure there are no obstacles in the way of the runners.

Ten Free Throws

Level of difficulty: moderate

This game is a good warm-up activity before playing basketball. It requires students to work in teams of five while shooting free throws.

EQUIPMENT
- One basketball for each team
- Basketball courts

GETTING STARTED:

Divide the students into teams of five, and assign each team a basket. Have each team stand single file behind the free throw line. Give each team a basketball.

RULES:

The first student in each line will shoot the ball at the basket, retrieve it, pass it to the second student in line, and then jog to the end of the line. The second player will complete the same tasks. Each time a student makes a basket, his or her team must call out the number of baskets the team has made up to that point. This relay continues until one team has made 10 free-throw baskets. For younger students, move the shooting line closer to the basket. For older students, give time constraints for completing the 10 baskets.

SAFETY PRECAUTIONS

Only the shooter may retrieve the ball.

Time Bomb

Level of difficulty: moderate

This is a variation of the over-under relay. It is played in groups of five to six students.

EQUIPMENT
- One medium-sized ball per group
- Whistle

GETTING STARTED:

Divide the students into groups of five or six. Have each group stand in a circle with at least an arm's length between each student. Give each group a ball.

RULES:

When the whistle is blown, each group will bounce pass its ball around the circle. To bounce pass, a student will hold the ball with both hands at waist level and face the student next to him or her. The "bouncer" pushes the ball forward and down from the waist and releases it. It will bounce on the ground halfway between the two players. When the whistle is blown again, each student holding a ball must freeze. The other members of the team must line up behind the student with the ball. When everyone is in line, the ball will be passed over the head, under the legs, or with a combination of over and under passes, until it reaches the last student in line. The last student must then run to the front of the line with the ball and begin the passing pattern over again. This will continue until each student in the group has been at the front of the line at least once.

SAFETY PRECAUTIONS

Spread the groups apart to avoid collisions.

Total Movement Relay

Level of difficulty: moderate

This relay involves teams of five or six players working together to complete a group movement exercise.

EQUIPMENT
- none needed

GETTING STARTED:

Divide the students into teams of five or six players. Have each team form a circle by holding hands. Have one team member stand in the center of the circle.

RULES:

Each team will travel from the starting line to a designated turnaround point. When the team returns to the starting line, the student in the middle of the circle will trade places with one of the students forming the circle. The students forming the circle must hold hands throughout the course, and they may not touch the student in the middle. The team will then travel across the playing area again. The game is completed when each student has had a turn to be in the middle of the circle.

SAFETY PRECAUTIONS

Do not allow the students to run.

Train Relays

Level of difficulty: moderate

Train relays involve teams of five players running a course with each player keeping his or her hands on the person in front of him or her.

EQUIPMENT
- A dozen plastic cones

GETTING STARTED:

Divide the students into teams of five. Have each team stand single file behind a designated starting line. Have the students place their hands on the shoulders of the students in front of them. Use plastic cones to mark the course through which the students will run.

RULES:

Each team will run through the designated course. The team members will keep their hands on the students in front of them at all times. When the team returns to the starting line, the student in the front of the *train* will run to the back and become the *caboose*. The relay will continue until each student has been at both the front and the end of the line.

SAFETY PRECAUTIONS

Caution the students to run carefully so that they will not trip over one another.

Pass and Duck Relay

Level of difficulty: challenging

This relay develops ball-handling skills and eye-hand coordination. It is played in groups of five students.

EQUIPMENT
- One medium-sized ball for each team
- Chalk

GETTING STARTED:

Use chalk to draw two parallel lines, five feet apart from each other, on the playground. Divide the students into groups of five. Have each group line up side by side or single file behind one of the lines. Designate the first student in each line to be the group's leader. Have each leader stand on the opposite line and face his or her group. Give each leader a ball.

RULES:

The leader will hold the ball with two hands at chest level. He or she will pass the ball to the first person in line by pushing the ball forward from the chest and releasing it. The first player in line will pass the ball back to the leader in the same manner and then duck down low to the ground. The leader will then pass the ball to the second player in line. The second player will pass the ball back and duck down. This process continues until the last player in line has passed the ball back to the leader. The leader will then go to the end of the line. The first player in line will become the new leader. The relay continues until the team is back to its original positions.

SAFETY PRECAUTIONS

Caution the students to watch the ball carefully, so that they do not get hit by it.

INDIVIDUAL FITNESS ACTIVITIES

Individual fitness activities focus on the students performing tasks at their own rates. The entire class participates in the particular activity at the same time, yet each student will complete the activity without the help of other students. The focus of these activities is to create a noncompetitive atmosphere in which every student is challenged to complete the activity to the best of his or her own ability.

These activities are designed around the important fitness concepts of building strength and endurance. They normally require a minimum amount of equipment. These tasks are easy to teach, require active participation, and should be fun for all involved.

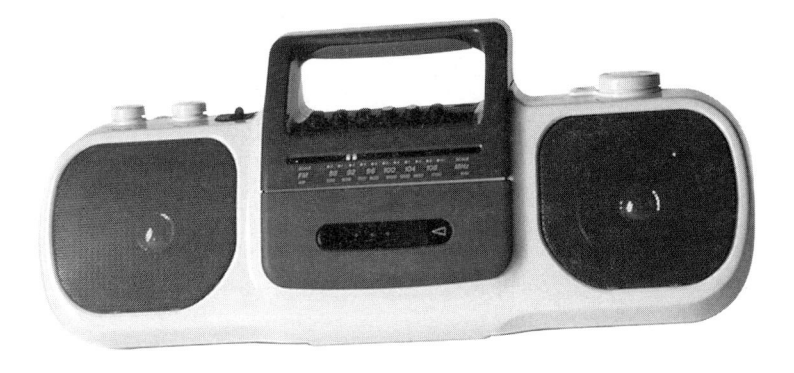

Around the Block

Level of difficulty: simple

This simple fitness activity is designed to build endurance.

EQUIPMENT
- Four plastic cones
- Four large index cards
- Tape
- Whistle

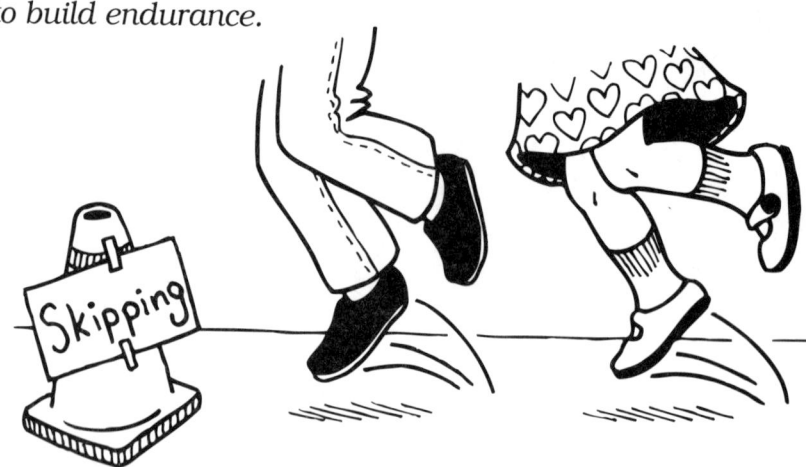

GETTING STARTED:

Arrange four plastic cones in a square with about 30 feet on each side. Select four exercises such as skipping, hopping, jogging, and jumping, and write each exercise on a separate index card. Tape each index card to a separate cone. Divide the students into four groups, and have each group line up at a separate cone.

RULES:

Students will move around the square in a counterclockwise direction. On each side of the square, the students will perform the exercise that is written on the card attached to that side's cone. When the whistle is blown, the students must stop and wait for a direction to complete a specific number of other exercises such as 10 abdominal crunches, 15 push-ups, or 20 jumping jacks. After those exercises are completed, the students will change directions and move clockwise around the square until they hear the whistle. Each group should be on a new side. The students will then complete the exercises written on the index cards, and additional exercises, until all four exercises are performed.

SAFETY PRECAUTIONS

Be sure that the students change tasks on each side of the square and that they have enough space to move in.

Freeze Dance

Level of difficulty: simple

Freeze Dance is a fun lead-in activity to a full aerobics lesson. It is ideal for younger students.

EQUIPMENT
- Tape recorded music
- Portable tape recorder

GETTING STARTED:

Have the students spread out over a large playing area.

RULES:

When the music begins, the students will dance in any way that they choose. Periodically stop the music. When the music stops, the students must freeze. Call out the names of any students who are seen moving. Those students will then move to the side of the playing area and will help judge if students move. Begin the music again, and tell the remaining students to resume dancing. Repeat the process until only a few students are left in the playing area.

SAFETY PRECAUTIONS
Use a large unobstructed playing area.

Hula-Hoops

Level of difficulty: simple

Hula-Hoops provide an endless number of activities and skills for students of any level.

EQUIPMENT
- One Hula-Hoop per student

GETTING STARTED:

Allow each student several minutes to practice twirling a hoop around his or her waist.

PROCEDURES:

Demonstrate how to twirl a hoop on the arm, neck, and waist. Invite the students to practice these movements. Hold a contest to see who can keep a hoop twirling for the longest time. Then have the students toss their hoops into the air and catch them. Challenge the students to try to put a spin on the hoops when they toss them. Hold another contest to see who can toss a hoop the highest. Use the hoops for other fitness activities. For example, have each student place a hoop on the ground. Then have the student run around it, skip around it, gallop around it, and so on. Give each student a ruler, and see if he or she can walk while using the ruler to keep the hoop moving alongside him or her. Finally, ask the students to come up with their own hoop activities.

SAFETY PRECAUTIONS

Students should twirl their hoops in a controlled fashion.

In, Out, and Around

Level of difficulty: simple

This is a fun activity that allows the students to practice moving safely while performing basic skills around Hula-Hoops.

EQUIPMENT
- One Hula-Hoop per student
- Whistle

GETTING STARTED:

Scatter the Hula-Hoops on the ground around a designated playing area. Have the students stand within the playing area.

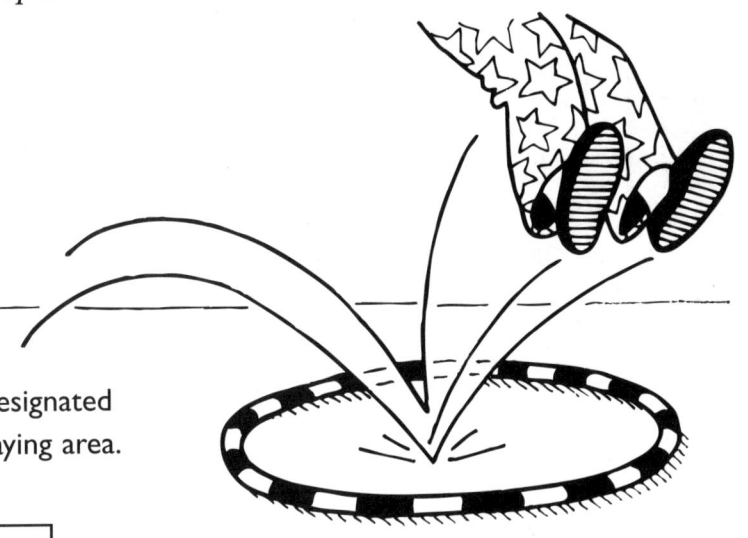

RULES:

When the whistle is blown one time, the students must move around the playing area without touching the hoops. Students may be asked to walk, jog, skip, hop, or perform a variety of movements during this time. When the whistle is blown two times, each student will find a hoop and jump in and out of the hoop until the next whistle. Each student must have his or her own hoop for this. When the whistle is blown three times in a row, each student will run around the outside of a hoop. Alternate the whistle commands throughout the activity.

SAFETY PRECAUTIONS

Warn the students to be careful of others as they move throughout the playing area. Make sure that there is only one student per hoop when the students are performing the jumping and running skills.

Jump and Jog

Level of difficulty: simple

Jump and Jog is a fun aerobic activity that keeps every student in constant motion.

EQUIPMENT
- Several plastic cones
- One jump rope for every two students
- Whistle

GETTING STARTED:

Place the cones in a large circle. Divide the students into two equal groups. Have one group stand in the middle of the circle. Give each student in that group a jump rope. Have the other group spread out around the outside of the circle.

RULES:

To begin the activity, blow the whistle. Each student in the middle of the circle will begin jumping rope. The students on the outside of the circle will jog around the circle. After one minute, blow the whistle again, and tell the students to stop moving. Then each student on the outside of the circle will trade places with a student in the middle of the circle. Blow the whistle again, and the students on the inside of the circle will jump rope and those on the outside will jog. The activity will continue until each student has jumped rope and jogged several times.

SAFETY PRECAUTIONS

Make the circle large enough so that there is plenty of room for the students to jump rope safely.

Jump Ropes

Level of difficulty: simple

Jump ropes provide students with opportunities to be creative and to progress at individual rates while building strength and endurance.

EQUIPMENT
- One jump rope per student
- Music (optional)

GETTING STARTED:

Give each student a jump rope. Play music, if it is available, to help motivate the students.

PROCEDURES:

Demonstrate, or ask students to demonstrate, how to perform jump-rope tricks such as single jumps, double jumps, jumping on one leg, jumping on alternating legs, and so on. Allow the students time to practice each skill. Then challenge them to work in small groups to develop jumping routines. Allow each group to demonstrate and teach its routine to the other groups.

SAFETY PRECAUTIONS

Allow for an adequate amount of space. Remind students to use caution when jumping rope around others.

Jump the River

Level of difficulty: simple

Jump the River is a simple activity in which the students practice jumping skills while pretending to jump over a river. This activity works best when the students are divided into groups of five to eight.

EQUIPMENT
- Two jump ropes per group

GETTING STARTED:

Divide the students into groups of five to eight. For each group, place two jump ropes on the ground so that they are parallel to each other and about one foot apart. Instruct each group to stand in line behind one of its jump ropes. Tell the students to pretend that the jump ropes are on the banks of a river, and that their task is to jump over the "river" without "getting wet" (or completely jumping over the ropes without touching them).

RULES:

The first student in line will try to jump over both ropes in a single jump. He or she may take a running start. If the student jumps completely over both ropes without touching them, he or she will walk to the end of the line. If the student lands between the two ropes or touches one of the ropes while jumping, he or she will sit off to the side until the next round begins. After each student has taken a turn at jumping over the river, the students will make the river wider by moving one of the jump ropes back one foot. This will continue until there is only one student left that has successfully jumped over the river without getting wet. Then the students will return the ropes to their original positions, and they will begin a new round with all of the students in the group participating.

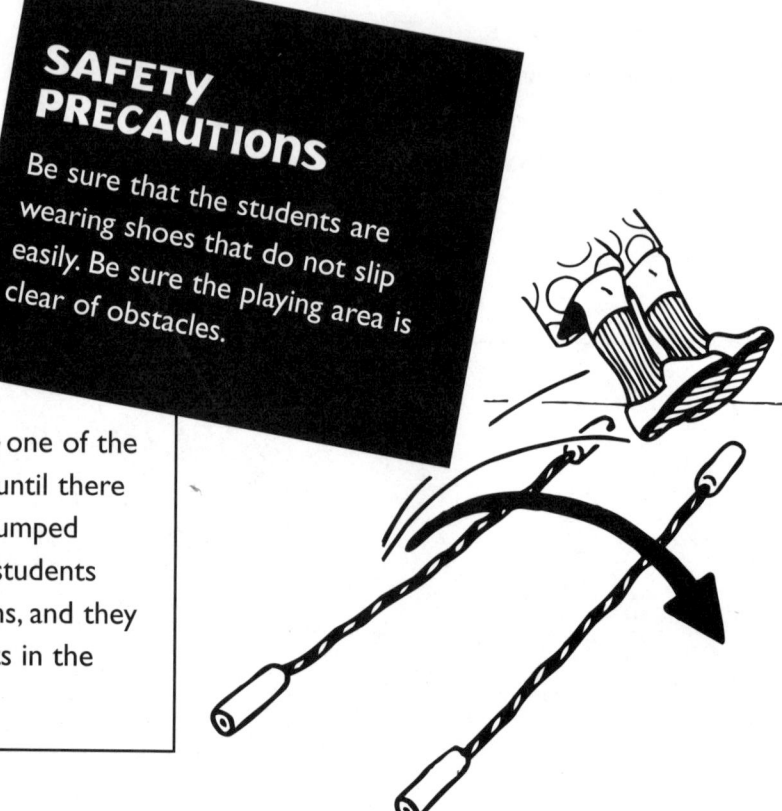

SAFETY PRECAUTIONS

Be sure that the students are wearing shoes that do not slip easily. Be sure the playing area is clear of obstacles.

Shuttle Run

Level of difficulty: simple

Shuttle Run is an aerobic activity that can be easily modified for any age group.

EQUIPMENT
- Two plastic cones per group

GETTING STARTED:

Divide the students into groups of four. Have each group stand single file along the end line of a basketball court. Use plastic cones to extend each free throw line from one sideline to the other.

RULES:

The first student in each group will run from the end line to the nearest free throw line (first cone). The student will then turn and run back to the starting line. The same student will then run to the center line of the basketball court and back to the starting line. He or she will then run to the far free throw line (second cone) and back, and finally to the opposite end line and back. When the student returns to the starting line after completing the run, he or she will go to the end of the group's line, and the next student in line will begin the shuttle run. This will continue until everyone has completed the run.

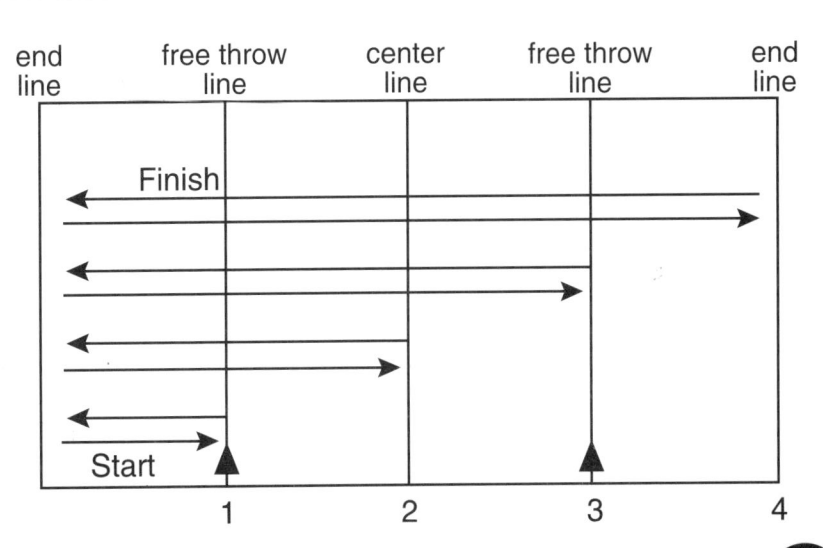

SAFETY PRECAUTIONS

Remind the students to run at a moderate pace so that they do not become overly tired.

Aerobics

Level of difficulty: simple to moderate

Aerobic activities can be used at any grade level. They can be personalized to suit any teaching style and any fitness-ability level.

EQUIPMENT
- Music (if available)

GETTING STARTED:

Lead the students out to a large area, preferably a soft, grass field. Explain to the class that you will be leading them in aerobic exercises and that they should follow you. If possible, use music to help motivate the students.

PROCEDURES:

The lesson should be divided into three sections: the warmup, the aerobic workout, and the cooldown. The warmup should last about 7 minutes, with 5 minutes of stretches and about 2 minutes of jogging in place. (This timing can vary according to age and ability; however, it is essential that students stretch thoroughly before exercising.) Begin the warmup with slow music. Lead the students through slow stretching exercises. You can refer to the stretching section of this book for various warmups. Hold each stretch for 10 seconds. After 5 minutes of stretches, end the warmup by having the students jog in place for about 2 minutes. Instruct them to jog with their knees high and their arms pumping. With this, the students should be sufficiently warmed up!

The aerobic workout should last about 5 to 20 minutes, depending on the age and ability of the class. If you are following along to music, you may want to use music with a quick tempo and upbeat sound. Remind students that they must stay in constant motion. The following is a list of recommended exercises for the full aerobic section of the lesson. Select the number of exercises to be performed based on the level of your class. If you run out of exercises, feel free to go back and repeat movements.

Jumping jacks: Jump and spread feet shoulder-width apart while touching hands overhead. Then jump and bring arms down to the side and feet together simultaneously.

Jumping jacks with legs only: Place hands on hips and move only legs as described for jumping jacks.

Biceps arm press: Begin with elbows bent at waist level; then curl arms up to chest.

Front-arm press: Press arms straight out in front, then pull them back. Press arms overhead, then pull them down.

Front-arm punch: Punch one arm, then the other, straight out in front of the body.

Straight-up arm punch: Alternate arms punching straight overhead.

Hopping: Hop in place with both feet.

One-foot hop: Alternate hopping on one foot.

Knee lunge: Step forward with one leg and bend the forward knee. Then stand up, step back, and repeat with the other leg.

Elbow squeeze: Raise arms so that the elbows are at chin level and squeeze elbows together in and out.

Side bends: Bend from the waist to the right. Reach toward the ground with the right hand. Repeat stretches, alternating sides.

High kicks: Kick leg straight up in the air. (Be careful not to swing the leg.) Alternate legs.

High kicks and high arms: Extend arm over head while kicking the opposite leg.

Triceps extensions: Extend elbows over head. Keeping the elbows close to the head, extend arms to touch hands and then lower arms.

Toe raises: Stand with legs straight and raise up on toes and back down again.

Elbow-to-knee touch: Alternate lifting knees while touching each knee with the opposite elbow.

Knee slaps: Alternate lifting knees while touching each leg with both hands as it rises.

Aerobics

Begin the cooldown section of the class by returning to slower music or instructing the students to slow down. Have the students walk slowly around the play area. Instruct them to take longer steps and to swing their arms in a controlled fashion.

After one minute, lead the students in cooldown stretches. Tell the students to stand on their tiptoes and stretch their arms high above their heads. Then have them bend at the waist to one side and then to the opposite side. Next, instruct the students to lie flat on their backs and stretch their arms over their heads. Then have students bend one knee, pull it to the chest, and then stretch it up straight in the air. Repeat with the other leg. Finally, have the students squat in a crouched position with their hands at their ankles. Now instruct them to slowly roll their bodies up until they are standing up straight with their arms at their sides.

SAFETY PRECAUTIONS

Allow enough room for students to work freely. If a student becomes short of breath, instruct him or her to walk slowly around the perimeter of the playing area for a few minutes. If the student is still out of breath, have him or her sit down and rest.

Fitness Circuits

Level of difficulty: simple to moderate

These simple fitness activities offer a well-rounded aerobic lesson, keeping students of any age involved and motivated.

EQUIPMENT
- Eight plastic cones
- Eight large index cards
- Whistle

GETTING STARTED:

Place eight cones about 10 feet apart in a circle on the playground. Write the name of a fitness activity on each index card. Activities may include jogging in place, jumping jacks, abdominal crunches, push-ups, and so on. Tape an index card to each cone. Divide the students into eight equal-sized groups.

RULES:

Each group will start at a specific cone. The members in the group will perform the activity written on the index card. After two to three minutes, blow the whistle. Each group must then move in a clockwise direction to the next station in the circle.

SAFETY PRECAUTIONS

Leave enough space between each station so that the students will not run into each other.

Name Game

Level of difficulty: simple to moderate

This activity allows students to move throughout a playing area, creating paths that form the shapes of letters and numbers.

EQUIPMENT
- none needed

GETTING STARTED:

Have the students spread out in a large, open space.

PROCEDURES:

Instruct the students to use their arms to "sky-write" their names in the air. Next, instruct each student to walk around the playing area and create paths that form the letters of his or her name. Challenge the student to create the same paths while running. For a variation, have the students hop, skip, or crab-walk the paths. Finally, have the students practice creating paths using numbers. Once they become proficient at forming the number paths, call out addition and subtraction problems. Each student should then form the paths for the problems as well as the answers to the problems.

SAFETY PRECAUTIONS

Caution the students to pay attention to where they are moving so that they do not run into one another.

Obstacle Courses

Level of difficulty: simple to moderate

Obstacle courses provide exciting opportunities for students to participate in an endless array of fitness skill activities. They can be put together in any playing area and easily modified for any grade and skill level.

EQUIPMENT
- Equipment varies with each type of course design.

GETTING STARTED:

Carefully assess the equipment and play areas that are available. Designate a clearly marked starting line and a finish line. Design a course for the students to move through that requires many different balance, coordination, movement, and aerobic skills. The following list includes suggestions for activities to include in the obstacle course:

- hop through a series of Hula-Hoops
- run around obstacles
- crawl under obstacles
- walk on a straight line or low balance beam
- dribble a ball from one place to another
- jump rope a given number of times
- slide down a slide (if available)
- throw a Frisbee at an object
- hit a tetherball around the pole (if available)
- bounce a tennis ball on a racket
- dribble a soccer ball around cones

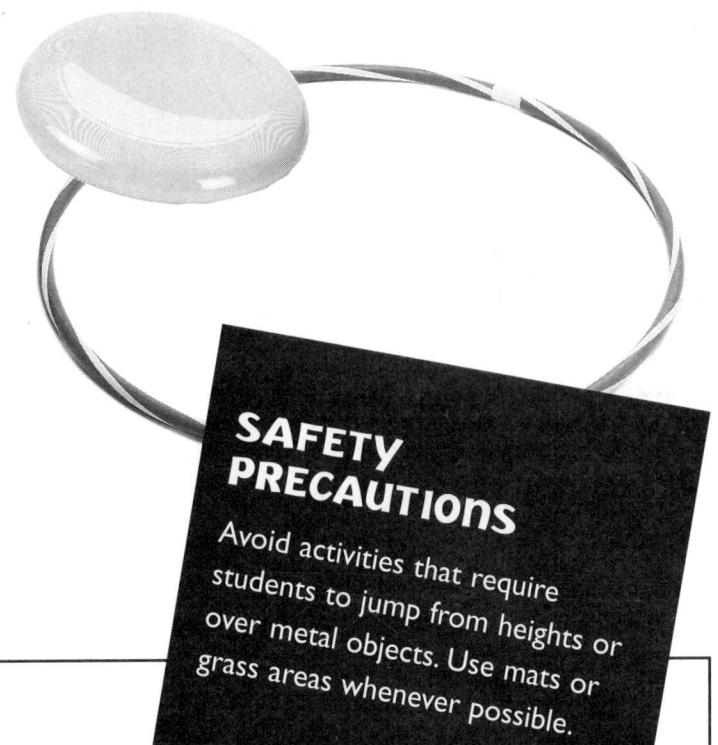

SAFETY PRECAUTIONS

Avoid activities that require students to jump from heights or over metal objects. Use mats or grass areas whenever possible.

PROCEDURES:

Have the students line up behind the starting line. Allow the first student in line to begin moving through the obstacle course. After he or she has completed the first or second activity, allow the next student in line to begin the course. Continue until all of the students have completed the course. Have each student who completes the course sit down in an area near the finish line until the rest of the students cross the finish line.

Track and Field

Level of difficulty: simple to moderate

Track and field skills are an important part of any fitness program. Students challenge themselves in running, jumping, and throwing events over the course of several lessons. The students should work at the different skills in small groups.

EQUIPMENT

- Chalk
- Several plastic cones
- Batons or chalkboard erasers
- Yardstick or tape measure
- Several softballs
- Several plastic disks (or Frisbees)
- Stopwatch

GETTING STARTED:

Use plastic cones to designate a large playing area. Explain to the students that they will be participating in running, jumping, and throwing events. Measure off the distances for each running event, and place cones at the starting lines and the finish lines. Use chalk to mark distances in feet or meters for the long jump events. Divide the students into small groups. Have the students complete a warmup and stretching routine before participating in any of the track and field events.

PROCEDURES:

Older students may be able to complete the assigned events as individual fitness stations. Younger students should be kept together with each group completing an event one at a time. Use a stopwatch to time the running events. Have each group complete the following activities:

Running Events

- 100-meter dash
- 200-meter run
- 400-meter run
- 400-meter relay—In this event each student on a four-member team runs 100 meters while carrying a baton. At the end of 100 meters, he or she hands off the baton to the next member on the team.

Jumping Events

- Standing long jump—Each student may jump three times. One student stands behind the starting line, swings his or her arms, and jumps forward, keeping both feet together. Mark the landing point with chalk or a plastic cone. Record the student's personal best distance.

- Running long jump—Each student may jump three times. One student stands several feet away from the starting line and takes a running start. When the student reaches the starting line, he or she jumps forward. Mark the landing point with chalk or a plastic cone. Record the student's personal best distance.

Throwing Events

- Softball throw—Each student may throw a softball three times. The student must stand behind the starting line and throw the softball as far as possible. Mark the landing point of the softball with chalk or a plastic cone. Record the student's personal best throw.

- Frisbee throw—Each student simulates the discus throw by using a plastic disk (or Frisbee). The student may throw the disk three times. He or she must stand behind the starting line. Then the student holds the disk with the thumb on top and fingers underneath. He or she bends the elbow, brings the disk into the body, spins around and releases the disk in front of the body. Mark the landing point with chalk or a plastic cone. Record the student's personal best throw.

SAFETY PRECAUTIONS

Allow for an adequate amount of space for each activity. Students participating in throwing activities should stand behind the thrower at all times.

Sportsfest

Level of difficulty: simple to moderate

An excellent way to get students excited about fitness is to implement a yearly Sportsfest competition. This is quite effective in promoting school spirit and camaraderie among the students and the faculty. It can also be a great way to end your physical education program as the culmination of a year's worth of progress in P.E.

PLANNING:

The first step in creating Sportsfest is to promote interest for it within the school. Send out a flyer to all of the teachers, aides, and administrators within the school inviting them to be a part of a Sportsfest Organizing Committee. Hold a meeting with the interested volunteers. At this meeting, explain that you would like to plan this event for the school and that the committee needs to decide on a date for the competition, coordinate the teams, decide what events to include in the competition, choose event coordinators, and choose the awards that will be given. (You may want to plan several meetings to space these decisions apart.)

The first task of the Sportsfest Organizing Committee is to choose the date(s) of the event. Check with administrators to see if the program will conflict with important school business. The event should be held in the afternoon after the day's academic tasks are complete, and it should not last more than two hours. Students may lose interest and become bored if the event goes much longer. Finally, be sure to plan a rain date in case of bad weather.

Organizing teams is also a priority for the committee. The simplest way to create teams is to separate the participants by grade level. Each grade could hold its own Sportsfest on separate days. If resources allow, you may want to consider holding an all-school event with all grades participating in separate events in one day. Whatever the case, divide the grades into two separate teams with members intermingled from different classrooms. The two teams can be named according to school colors or mascots, which is a great way to promote school spirit.

The committee must also determine the number and type of activities for the competition. Include running events such as the 100-meter dash, the 200-meter run, and a four-person 100-meter relay. An ideal situation would be to have an existing running track for the events. If this is not available, it will be necessary to measure and mark the running distances on the playground or field. (At least three people should supervise each running event, with one person at the starting line, one at the finish line, and one to record the results.) Other events such as the long jump, three-legged race, tug-of-war (use a strong rope on a soft surface), potato-sack race, and softball shotput toss (make sure participants are standing behind the thrower) should also be considered. Finally, review this book for other possible activities to include, such as a soccer game.

Once the events have been selected, determine how many participants should be in each event. Generally, all students should participate in at least two events. Allow students to sign up for the events they would like to do. If some events prove more popular than others, draw names out of a hat or use some other kind of random selection to choose participants.

The next task is to choose event coordinators. These individuals will be in charge of supervising and keeping track of scores for each event. Generally, teachers are ideal for these positions, but you can enlist help from the community. Sometimes area high schools can be an excellent resource for student volunteers. The same people can supervise all of the events if necessary. Use your own discretion as to who and how many will supervise each event.

The committee should also decide on how events will be scored. There could be a first-, second-, and third-place winner for each event, with these winners each given an individual award. In addition to the individual awards, the teams of those winners can be awarded points: a first-place finish should earn 15 points, a second-place finish 10 points, and a third-place finish 5 points. The overall score of each team can be determined by totaling the number of points its members earn during each event. It is important to keep detailed track of these scores. Devise a chart to record scores for each event, and distribute copies to the event supervisors. During the actual events, excitement will grow as coordinators tally the scores and the students learn of their teams' progress.

Sportsfest

Plan to hold an awards ceremony for the day's participants after the events are over. If possible, obtain a public address system and announce the names and teams of the top three finishers in each event. Honor the student with the highest number of individual points as the Most Valuable Player of the day. Once individual achievements are cited, read each team's total number of points, ending with the top points-earning team.

The awards you distribute can be trophies, medals, certificates, ribbons, or anything else you can think of. Awards should be given to the first-, second-, and third-place winners, and a certificate of participation should be given to every competitor. Some kind of token can also be given to the members of the winning team; however, usually the excitement of winning will be enough. The kinds of awards that can be given out will depend on the budget the committee has to spend. Sometimes it is possible to solicit donations from outside sources, such as a sporting goods store, a trophy shop, or a larger sports organization. (Check with school administrators before contacting outside sources for donations.) All awards must be ordered and received before the final event.

Finally, consider how to promote Sportsfest. In order to help motivate the students, begin advertising the event a month in advance. Create colorful flyers and posters announcing Sportsfest. Send the flyers home to parents and put the posters up around the school. Ask for student volunteers to help decorate the field with balloons, posters, or banners. You can even organize an informal pep rally for the teams right before the start of Sportsfest.

THE BIG DAY:

Once the day of the event arrives, all of your diligent planning will create a day of fun, excitement, and celebration. Double-check that the volunteers are in place, the teachers know where to bring the students, the competitors are prepared to compete, and the awards are ready to be handed out.

Sportsfest can be a great experience for both students and faculty. This can be an extremely successful event that builds both team and school spirit while introducing the students to the excitement of organized athletics! Have fun!

Bowling

Level of difficulty: moderate

This is a fun imitation of bowling that involves setting up milk cartons on the playground and rolling a ball to knock them down. It can be played in groups of four to six students.

EQUIPMENT

For each group:
- Ten empty quart-sized milk cartons
- One medium-sized rubber ball
- Chalk
- Paper, pencil, clipboard (optional)

GETTING STARTED:

It is important to plan ahead for this activity. Ask the students to bring in empty milk cartons well in advance to ensure that there are enough cartons available for each group. Separate the students into small groups. Give each group 10 milk cartons and one ball. Instruct the group to set the cartons up in front of a fence or wall as illustrated here.

RULES:

Draw a line approximately 15 feet from the milk cartons. One student will stand behind the line and roll the ball toward the cartons. He or she will get two attempts at knocking down all of the cartons. The remaining students in the group will take turns both retrieving the ball for the student who is bowling and resetting the cartons for the next student to bowl.

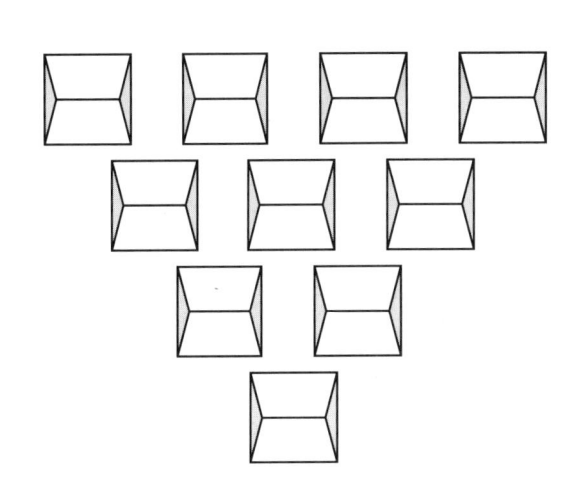

Bowling

Keeping Score: Older students may be interested in learning how to keep score. If so, reproduce the scoresheet on page 103, and distribute a copy to each group, along with a clipboard and a pencil.

Use the sample scoresheet below to demonstrate how to fill out the scoresheet.

Name	1	2	3	4	5	6	7	8	9	10	Total
Carole	X / 20	7/ / 40	X / 60	8/ / 80	X / 100	9/ / 120	X / 140	9/ / 160	X / 180	9/ x / 200	200
Cedric	X / 30	X / 60	X / 90	X / 120	X / 150	X / 180	X / 210	X / 240	X / 270	X X X / 300	300
Amy	7 2 / 9	9 - / 18	X / 37	7/ 2 / 46	7/ / 66	X / 86	7/ / 105	9/ / 124	9/ / 144	9/ x 9 / 164	164
Juan	7/ / 17	7/ / 32	5/ / 51	9/ / 69	8/ / 88	9/ / 106	8/ / 123	7/ / 142	9/ / 159	7 / 9 / 178	178

Have the students in each group write their names on the scoresheet in the order in which they will bowl. Each bowler will complete 10 frames. If a bowler knocks down all of the cartons with one roll of the ball, he or she scores a *strike*. A strike is worth 10 points plus the total number of cartons knocked down by the bowler's next two rolls of the ball. To indicate a strike, the bowler marks an X in the first box in the upper right-hand corner of the larger box on the scoresheet for that frame. The final score for that frame is written in after the next two balls are rolled. A *spare* is scored when a bowler knocks down all 10 cartons with two rolls of the ball. A spare is worth 10 points plus the number of pins knocked down with the first ball thrown in the bowler's next frame. The bowler marks a diagonal line through the second box in the corner of the larger box on the scoresheet for a spare. The final score for that frame is recorded after the bowler rolls the first ball of his or her next frame. Then the number of cartons knocked down with that ball is added to the 10 points previously scored for the spare, and the sum is written in the larger box. If the bowler does not roll a strike or a spare, he or she only counts the number of cartons knocked down within that frame. The number of cartons knocked down with the first roll is written in the first box and the number of cartons knocked down with the second roll is written in the second box for that frame. If no cartons are knocked over, a dash is drawn through the small box for that frame. The score does not carry over to the next turn.

SAFETY PRECAUTIONS

Students waiting for their turns should stand off to the side of the cartons or behind the bowler.

Name	1	2	3	4	5	6	7	8	9	10	Total

Racket Skills

Level of difficulty: moderate to challenging

Racket skills are ideal for working on eye-hand coordination.

EQUIPMENT
- One tennis racket or table tennis paddle per student
- One tennis ball per student
- Handball walls, tennis nets, or volleyball nets

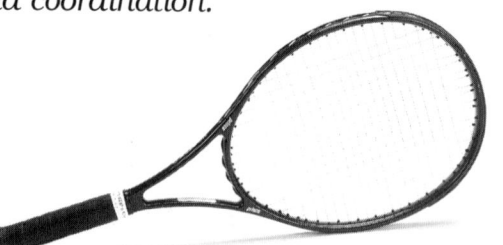

SAFETY PRECAUTIONS
Students should not swing the rackets over their heads. They may never hit another person with a racket. Be sure to have enough space for the students to work in to avoid overcrowding.

GETTING STARTED:
Give each student a racket and a tennis ball.

PROCEDURES:
Have each student complete the following series of racket skills.

- Hold the racket and balance the ball on it.
- Move the ball around the racket without letting it fall off.
- Balance the ball on the racket while walking.
- Bounce the ball on the racket while standing still.
- Bounce the ball on the racket while walking.
- Bounce the ball high up into the air with the racket.
- Count how many times you can bounce the ball on the racket before the ball drops to the ground.
- Practice hitting the ball against a wall.
- Practice hitting the ball back and forth with a partner.
- Hit the ball over a net and to a partner. Count the number of times the ball is hit back and forth.

PLAYGROUND GAMES

There are many games and activities that have been played on playgrounds for generations. Some of these games require existing playground equipment, but many require only a little imagination and a few painted lines or plastic cones.

These games have been passed down from child to child over the years. The children usually know how to play most of the games, and can probably teach adults a few things about the intricacies of a given game. There may be some variations to the rules due to regional differences so it will be helpful to review the rules and skills of the games with the children.

Although these games are "built-in" to the playground or park, they can be incorporated into any physical education program. They all require specific fitness skills, and most can be used as lead-up activities for other games. The students will enjoy having the opportunity to improve their skills in playground games.

Handball

Level of difficulty: simple

Handball is a simple playground game that requires eye-hand coordination and can be modified to be more challenging to older students.

EQUIPMENT

- One medium-sized rubber ball per group
- One handball court per group (If handball courts are not available, an unobstructed area of wall space can be used.)

GETTING STARTED:

Divide the students into the same number of groups as there are handball courts. Have each group stand in line a few feet away from its court. Give each group a ball. The first two players in line will stand on the court facing the wall.

RULES:

The player who begins the game is called the *server*. The server drops the ball on the ground and hits it with one palm after the first bounce. The ball must hit the wall before it bounces on the ground again. After the serve, the server's opponent must hit the ball before it bounces two times. The players then take turns hitting the ball against the wall. Players may not block each other from hitting the ball. When a player fails to return the ball before it bounces twice on the ground, he or she is out and must go to the end of the line. The next player in line will then play a challenge match against the winner.

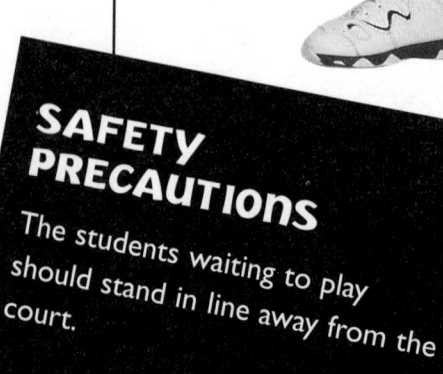

SAFETY PRECAUTIONS

The students waiting to play should stand in line away from the court.

Roly-poly

Level of difficulty: simple

This game is a safer variation of dodge ball. It involves half of the players rolling balls at the feet of the other half of the players.

EQUIPMENT
- Several small rubber balls or foam balls

GETTING STARTED:

Divide the students into two groups. Have one group form a large circle. Have the other group spread out inside the circle. Give several balls to the students forming the circle.

RULES:

Each player with a ball will roll the ball at the feet of the players inside the circle. The players inside the circle must try to avoid being hit by a ball. If a player is hit with a ball, he or she will become part of the group forming the circle. When no one is left in the center of the circle, the original teams will switch positions and start a new round.

A variation can be played in which a player in the circle will switch positions with the ball roller who hits him or her. This allows for continuous, uninterrupted play.

SAFETY PRECAUTIONS

Do not allow the students to throw the balls at each other.

Tetherball

Level of difficulty: simple

This is a popular one-on-one playground game. It requires eye-hand coordination.

EQUIPMENT
- Tetherball courts

GETTING STARTED:

Divide the students into the same number of groups as there are tetherball courts. Have each group stand in line beside a court.

RULES:

The first two players in line will stand at opposite sides of the pole from one another. One player starts the game by hitting the ball toward the other player. The second player hits the ball back toward the first player. Players may hit the ball using only one hand. They may not touch the rope or chain. The player who hits the ball over his or her opponent's head and winds the rope completely around the pole wins. The winning player stays in the court. The other player goes to the end of the line and is replaced by the next player in line.

SAFETY PRECAUTIONS

The students waiting in line for a turn should stand away from the pole and the players.

Four Corners

Level of difficulty: moderate

Four Corners is easy to play and involves endurance and attention skills.

EQUIPMENT
- Foursquare court painted on the playground for each group

GETTING STARTED:

Divide the students into groups of six to eight players. Have each group line up near a foursquare court. Have each of the first four people in line stand on a separate corner of their group's foursquare court facing in. The fifth person in line will stand in the center of the court.

RULES:

When the player in the center of the court calls out, "Go left" or "Go right," each player standing on a corner must move in that direction to the next corner. The person in the center must try to run to one of the corners before one of the other players. He or she is allowed three attempts to accomplish this task. If the player in the center cannot get to a corner within three tries, he or she will walk to the end of the group's line. The first person in the line will then stand in the center of the court and play will continue. If the person in the center beats another player to a corner, he or she will become a corner person. The other player will move to the end of the group's line.

SAFETY PRECAUTIONS

Do not allow more than five people in the court at any time. The players waiting for a turn must form a line away from the court.

Foursquare

This is a classic playground game involving eye-hand coordination.

Level of difficulty: moderate

EQUIPMENT
- One medium-sized rubber ball per group
- One foursquare court per group
- Chalk

GETTING STARTED:

Divide the students into groups of five to seven players. For each group, have one player stand in each quadrant of the foursquare court. Have the remaining players stand in a line away from the court. Use chalk to label the quadrants A, B, C, and D.

RULES:

The player in quadrant A will start the game by bouncing the ball on the ground and using the palms of the hands to hit the ball to any other player. The ball must bounce completely inside another quadrant without touching the boundary line. The ball will continue to be bounced and passed from one player to another until it touches or goes over a boundary line. At that point, the last person who touched the ball will leave the court and walk to the end of the line. The first person in the line will take his or her place.

The basic rules of Foursquare can be modified to create several versions of the game. One version is called *Around the World*. In this game, the players must bounce the ball around the square in succession to quadrants A, B, C, and D. If a player does not follow the pattern, he or she will walk to the end of the line and will be replaced with another player.

SAFETY PRECAUTIONS
Each student waiting for a turn to play must stand off to the side of the square.

Hopscotch

Level of difficulty: moderate

This game is a playground favorite that involves jumping and hopping skills. This is only one of the many ways that children play hopscotch.

EQUIPMENT
- One marker per student (Rocks, sticks, pieces of chalk, and other easy-to-find materials can be used as markers.)
- Hopscotch lines

GETTING STARTED:

Use existing hopscotch lines or draw them with chalk on the playground. Give each player a marker. Divide the students into groups of no more than five players. Have each group line up near its hopscotch lines.

RULES:

The first player will toss his or her marker into the first square. Standing on one foot, the player must hop over the first square and then into each of the following squares. The only time the player may put both feet down at the same time is in the double squares—4 and 5 and 7 and 8. When the player reaches the ninth square, he or she must turn around and hop back through the pattern. Upon returning to square two, the player will pick up his or her marker from square one while balancing on one foot, and then hop out of the pattern. If the player touches a line while hopping, he or she must step out of the pattern and go to the end of the line. That player will then wait until his or her next turn to attempt hopping through the pattern again. Each of the remaining players will take a turn completing this task. Then the process will begin again with each player tossing his or her marker into square two and hopping through the pattern. The first player to toss his or her marker into each square and to hop successfully through the pattern nine times wins.

SAFETY PRECAUTIONS
If hopping is too difficult for a student, allow him or her to jump with both feet.

111

FS-32601 Outdoor Play © Frank Schaffer Publications, Inc.

Prisoner

Level of difficulty: moderate

This is a popular playground game that can serve as a lead-in to playing volleyball. It is played with 6 to 10 players.

EQUIPMENT
- Volleyball net for every two teams
- Volleyball for every two teams

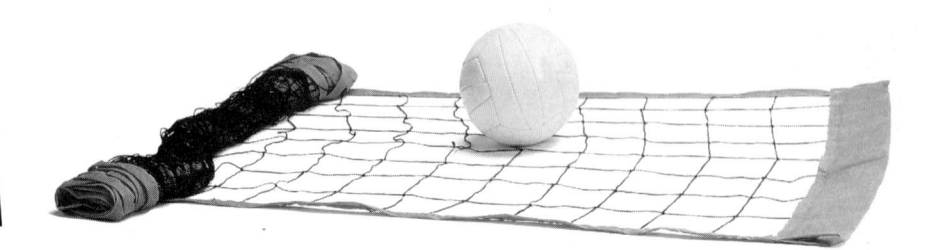

GETTING STARTED:

Divide the students into teams of 6 to 10 players. Have each team stand on one side of a volleyball court. Make sure that the students know the names of everyone on the court. Give one player a ball.

RULES:

The player with the ball will call out the name of a player on the opposite team and will then throw the ball over the net to that team. The ball must be thrown over the net and within the boundaries of the court, or the thrower will be sent to "jail." When a player goes to jail, he or she must stand off to the side of the court and form a jail line. Anyone on the receiving team may catch the ball; however, if the ball is dropped, the player whose name was called must go to jail. If the ball is caught, the player who caught it will then call the name of a player on the opposite team and will throw the ball back over the net. Each team may free the first person in its jail line by calling out "jailbreak" when a member of the team throws the ball over to the opposite team. If the opposing team drops the ball, then the throwing team's prisoner will be released from jail and allowed to come back onto the court. If the ball is caught, the prisoner will remain out of the game and the receiving team will take its turn. The game ends when a team has no players left on the court.

SAFETY PRECAUTIONS

To avoid congestion, do not allow more than 10 students on each side of the court.

Spud

Level of difficulty: moderate

Spud is a game that can be played with the entire class or in smaller groups. It involves running, catching, and eye-hand coordination skills.

EQUIPMENT
- Plastic cones or painted playground lines
- One medium-sized ball per group

GETTING STARTED:

Use plastic cones or painted playground lines to mark the boundaries of a large playing area. Have the students stand in the center of the playing area. Give a ball to one player.

RULES:

The player with the ball will throw the ball up in the air and all the students will run away from the center of the playing area. While the ball is in the air, the player who threw it will call out another player's name. The player whose name is called will turn around and try to catch the ball. If the player can't catch it, he or she will sit out for the rest of the round. If the ball is caught, the player will yell out "Spud!" and all the runners will freeze. The player with the ball will try to roll the ball so that it hits one of the frozen runners. He or she is allowed to take three steps in order to get closer to the target. If a frozen runner is hit with the ball, he or she will sit out for the rest of the round. If the player rolling the ball misses the target, he or she will sit out for the rest of the round. The remaining players will then reassemble in the center of the playing area and the entire sequence will be repeated. The round continues until only three people are left in the game. Then all the players will rejoin the game for another round.

SAFETY PRECAUTIONS

Make sure that the playing area is free of obstacles. Do not allow a student to throw the ball at other students.

PARACHUTE ACTIVITIES

A parachute is a wonderful piece of equipment that will enhance any physical education program. Parachutes can be purchased at some teacher supply stores or ordered through catalogs. Parachutes can also be purchased at Army surplus stores.

Parachute activities help to increase flexibility, build endurance, and increase arm and shoulder strength. Most importantly, these activities are fun for children of any age.

Level of difficulty: simple

The parachute activities described on the following pages will add an exciting and fun element to your physical education program.

EQUIPMENT
- One or more parachutes
- Additional equipment needed is listed with each activity.

GETTING STARTED:

Lay the parachute out on the ground and have the students spread out evenly around its perimeter. Have the students grip the edge of the parachute with both hands and lift it to waist level. Count to three and have the students lift the parachute over their heads and back down again. Allow the students to practice this several times. Then have the students practice shaking the parachute to create both large and small waves. Finally, have the students practice holding the parachute with one hand and walking around in a circle. Students can also practice skipping, hopping, and running around the circle while holding the parachute.

PROCEDURES:

Select five or six of the activities on the following pages for one class session. Each activity should last approximately five minutes. If time allows, encourage the students to repeat their favorite activities.

Popcorn

Have the students lay the parachute on the ground and sit around it. Place 15 to 20 small balls such as tennis balls, whiffle balls, and handballs on the parachute. Have each student grasp the edge of the parachute with both hands, stand up, and hold it at waist level. Then direct the students to shake the parachute until all of the balls bounce off it. Use the stopwatch to time how long it takes the students to complete this task. Challenge them to improve their time in subsequent rounds.

ADDITIONAL EQUIPMENT
- 15–20 small balls
- stopwatch

FS-32601 Outdoor Play © Frank Schaffer Publications, Inc.

PARACHUTE ACTIVITIES

Ball Roll

Have the students stand in a circle around the parachute, holding it at waist level. Place a medium-sized ball on the parachute. Challenge the students to roll the ball in a circle around the edge of the parachute without allowing it to fall on the ground. After the ball has completed several circles, direct the students to change its direction. Use the stopwatch to time how long the students can keep the ball rolling.

Create a Dome

During this activity, the students will make a dome shape with the parachute and sit inside of the dome. Begin by laying the parachute flat on the ground. Have the students stand in a circle around the parachute. Instruct the students to bend down and grip the edge of the parachute. Next, tell them to work in unison to raise the parachute as quickly as possible and as high over their heads as possible. As the parachute fills with air, urge the students to step forward, pulling the parachute behind their backs as they move forward, and then to sit on the inside edge of the parachute. When this activity is performed properly, the parachute should hold the air inside itself, creating a dome over the students' heads.

Riding the Waves

Have the students hold the parachute at waist level. Tell them to imagine that the parachute is a great ocean. Choose two students at a time to crawl under the ocean. After each student has had a chance to crawl under the parachute, repeat the activity, but allow the students to simulate ocean waves by shaking the parachute as the crawlers move beneath it.

ADDITIONAL EQUIPMENT
- one medium-sized ball
- stopwatch

Snake in the Grass

Instruct the students to lay the parachute flat on the ground. Choose one person to be the *snake in the grass*. The snake must lie flat on his or her stomach in the middle of the parachute. Have the remaining students spread out and stand on top of the parachute. (To help prevent injuries, have the students remove their shoes.) No one may step off the parachute. The snake must slither around on his or her stomach and try to tag the other students. When a student is tagged, he or she also becomes a snake. Play continues until all of the students have become snakes.

Floating Cloud

Have the students form a circle and hold the parachute at waist level. Instruct the students to bend down in unison, and then lift the parachute high over their heads while holding it tightly. Give a signal, such as a whistle blow, and have all of the students let go of the parachute at the same time. As the parachute floats through the air, the students will move to the middle of the circle and sit down. When the parachute lands, it will cover the students like a blanket.

Merry-Go-Round

Instruct the students to hold the parachute with one hand at waist level and face in the same direction. Assign specific movements such as walking, running, hopping, skipping, and galloping, and have the students perform each movement while still holding the parachute with one hand. Change the task for each rotation of the parachute. For variety, have the students hold the parachute at different levels while completing the various movements.

PARACHUTE ACTIVITIES

Changing Colors

Instruct the students to spread out around the parachute so that each student is holding on to a different color from that of his or her neighbor. Have the students raise the parachute over their heads. Then call out one of the parachute's colors. When the students hear the color they are holding, they must release the parachute and run underneath the parachute to another section of the same color. For example, if the color blue is called, all of the students holding a blue section will release the parachute, run to another blue section, and grip the edge of the parachute at the new section. Repeat this activity until every color is called at least twice.

Cat and Mouse

For safety reasons, this activity should be played on a grass field or a matted area, and will work best with younger children. Instruct the students to kneel on the ground while holding on to the parachute. Designate two or three students to be "mice" and one student to be the "cat." The mice will crawl around underneath the parachute, the cat will crawl on top of the parachute, and the remaining students will shake the parachute. The cat must try to tag all of the mice. When all of the mice have been tagged, pick different students as the cat and mice. Repeat until all of the students have had the chance to be either a cat or a mouse.

ADDITIONAL EQUIPMENT
- The parachute must be multicolored.

AWARDS AND FORMS

Using achievement awards and progress forms helps motivate students and increases their enjoyment of physical education. Achievement awards should be given to individual students for individual success. When used appropriately and sparingly, these awards can provide a positive boost to any student's self-esteem. Progress forms should be used quarterly to track each student's fitness skill development and personal interest in athletics.

ACHIEVEMENT AWARDS

Achievement awards should be given to students for personal achievement, good sportsmanship, and positive attitude. Receiving an individual award can help strengthen the confidence of any student. Children enjoy recognition and will be motivated to perform at a higher level when they know they have the opportunity to be singled out from their peers.

Try to present awards to no more than one or two students at a time. Consider presenting awards every week or two throughout the year so that students are continually aware of the opportunity to earn an award. Make sure that every student receives at least one award during the year. Present the certificates in front of the class and explain how the students earned their awards.

PROGRESS FORMS

Progress forms are useful tools for helping students follow their own fitness skill development. Encourage students to create fitness goals for themselves, and have them document their progress toward these goals by using the progress forms.

Easy-to-track fitness skills include endurance, flexibility, and strength. Provide an exercise chart on which students can record their initial skills. Then have them set goals for improving their skills. For example, they can record how many times they can hop on one foot at the beginning of the year, and then set a goal for increasing this number throughout the year.

Another useful tracking tool is an interest inventory. This provides a forum for students to explore their feelings about sports. Encourage them to describe their feelings about exercise and their feelings about themselves when they are engaged in sports and fitness activities. They can also use this tool to write out individual goals for a given time period.

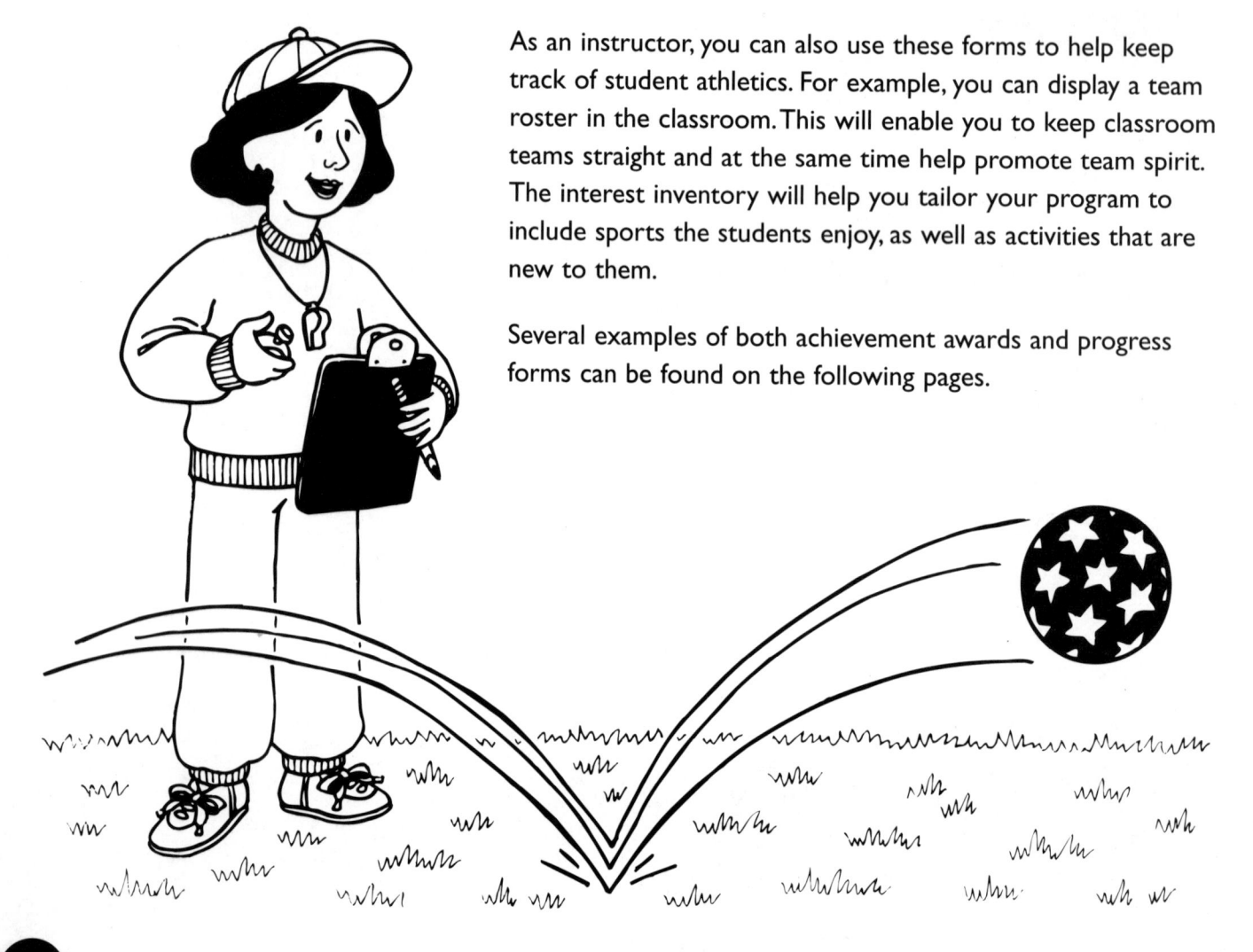

As an instructor, you can also use these forms to help keep track of student athletics. For example, you can display a team roster in the classroom. This will enable you to keep classroom teams straight and at the same time help promote team spirit. The interest inventory will help you tailor your program to include sports the students enjoy, as well as activities that are new to them.

Several examples of both achievement awards and progress forms can be found on the following pages.

What Are Your Physical Skills?

Name _____

Use the following form as an achievement record of your skills. Fill this in at the beginning of the year and the end of the year.

	Beginning of the year	**End of the year**
1. For how many minutes can you walk without stopping?	_____ minutes	_____ minutes
2. For how many minutes can you run without stopping?	_____ minutes	_____ minutes
3. How many times can you hop on your left foot?	_____ times	_____ times
4. How many times can you hop on your right foot?	_____ times	_____ times
5. How many times can you jump rope without missing?	_____ times	_____ times
6. How well can you throw a ball? (not so well, OK, very well)	_____	_____
7. How well can you catch a ball? (not so well, OK, very well)	_____	_____
8. How well can you bounce a ball? (not so well, OK, very well)	_____	_____
9. How well can you kick a ball? (not so well, OK, very well)	_____	_____
10. How often are you a good sport? (never, sometimes, always)	_____	_____

Interest Inventory

Grade _____

Name _____

Date _____

1. Do you like to play sports or do you prefer to watch them? Use the space below to write about your feelings toward sports.

   _____
   _____
   _____
   _____

2. Do you play any sports after school or on the weekends? List them here.

   _____
   _____

3. List some sports that you would like to learn to play here.

   _____
   _____

4. Choose a sport from one of the two lists above. Write some things that you know about that sport.

   _____
   _____
   _____
   _____

TEAM ROSTERS FOR

_____

Team Name
_____

Members
_____
_____
_____
_____
_____

Team Name
_____

Members
_____
_____
_____
_____
_____

Team Name
_____

Members
_____
_____
_____
_____
_____

Team Name
_____

Members
_____
_____
_____
_____
_____

Team Name
_____

Members
_____
_____
_____
_____
_____

Teacher: Fill in your classroom name (example: Room 11 or Ms. Butler's Class) and the various team names and team members. Display this form in the classroom to help students keep track of their teams for any sport your class plays repeatedly. Make copies and distribute to each student.

FS-32601 Outdoor Play © Frank Schaffer Publications, Inc.

Certificate

This Absolutely Certifies That

_____

has shown
Great Sportsmanship.

Date: _____

by _____

Certificate of Achievement

Awarded for excellence in Physical Education to

_____

on this date

_____

by

_____

Great Effort

in

Physical Education awarded to

_____

on this date _____

by _____